I0033777

ROAD TO DEBT FREEDOM

S. TODD COOK AND MICHAEL A. KIEFER

American Literary Press, Inc.
Five Star Special Edition
Baltimore, Maryland

ROAD TO DEBT FREEDOM

Copyright © 2000 S. Todd Cook and Michael A. Kiefer

All rights reserved under International and
Pan-American copyright conventions.
No part of this book may be reproduced, stored in a retrieval system, or
transmitted in any form, electronic, mechanical, or other means, now
known or hereafter invented, without written permission of the publisher.
Address all inquiries to the publisher.
Reasonable care has been exercised in preparing the text to insure its
clarity and accuracy. This book is sold with the understanding that the
authors and the publisher are not engaged in rendering legal, accounting,
or other professional services. State laws vary and readers with specific
financial questions should seek the services of a professional advisor.

Cover Concept: Ricardo Longoria
Illustrations: Ricardo Longoria

Library of Congress
Cataloging-in-Publication Data
ISBN 1-56167-630-6

Library of Congress Card Catalog Number:
00-104288

Sixth Printing

Published by

American Literary Press, Inc.
Five Star Special Edition
8019 Belair Road, Suite 10
Baltimore, Maryland 21236

Manufactured in the United States of America

DEDICATION

*May God bless Beverly Cook and our family members
who are no longer with us.
You are truly missed and loved.*

Special thanks to our families and friends, especially our parents Steve and Diane Cook & Dick and Carole Kiefer, who have always encouraged us to pursue our dreams.

A.N.P.—thanks for all you have done and for being a true friend.

Jana—thanks for always being supportive, understanding, and caring.

Brent—you are an inspiration and a true gift from God.

Liz—thanks for your commitment and for always being there.

Todd & Mike

Acknowledgements

This is our first book, which we hope to share with many individuals and families to help educate them to better comprehend and manage their personal finances. This book is a product resulting from our hands-on experience in the debt management field. It has taken many years to compile the material needed to complete this work. Without the help of our friends, co-workers, and associates this book would have never become a reality.

Many thanks to all the employees at American Literary Press, Inc. for making our first experience with a publisher exceptional. Your professionalism and commitment to this publication deserves many accolades. We would like to give a special acknowledgment to Julie, Donna, and Alan for their dedication throughout this project.

Ricardo Longoria, your imaginative mind and creative illustrations have helped provide a clear conveyance of our ideas.

To our readers, remember that it is possible to pave your Road To Debt Freedom. You have to choose the path that is right for you and remain committed. Once you get past a few obstacles that might be in the way, the ultimate goal of successfully managing and reducing your debt will be within reach.

S. Todd Cook
Michael A. Kiefer

INTRODUCTION

Congratulations!!!!! You have taken the first step in understanding and successfully reducing your debt. By opening this book, you have committed to the fact that getting out of debt concerns and interests you. We all have interests. Some people like sports, some like collecting things, and some others like computers or other hobbies. The people who are most successful in developing their interests are those who have experienced positive results in pursuit of their interests. Positive results tend to motivate and reaffirm the purpose of the idea or interest we are pursuing. Pursuing your interest in debt reduction can be an extremely fun and rewarding experience, through which you will see much progress. At times it will not be easy, and sacrifices will need to be made. No matter what our interests, we all at some point in our lives achieve some form of success. Along the way, there may be times that are confusing and may seem hopeless. Those who succeed use a positive attitude to persevere through the difficult times. We all have the ability to persevere, the ability to persevere manifests itself right from our infancy when, through trial and error, we learn to crawl, walk, and talk. Sometimes we fall down, but it is important that we get back on our feet and keep trying.

Everybody's road to success starts somewhere and not all of the successful roads terminate at the same point. Without assistance, starting the journey to becoming debt free is the biggest obstacle and will undoubtedly cause much frustration. You may feel lost or may not know what options are available. However, there is no risk in trying to become financially free, and if achieved, the rewards can be many. By opening this book, you have shown an interest in debt reduction. We realize that much like achieving any other type of accomplishment, success in debt reduction will require guidance and sharing of information from individuals who have worked with the same experiences. Reducing debt often requires changing your lifestyle or the way you relate to your finances and spending behavior.

One common theme you will experience on the road to becoming debt free is that planning, perseverance, and organization are the main ingredients to becoming financially free, and these ingredients do not cost a red cent. We believe this book will serve as a map to guide construction of your road to financial recovery. Using it will assist you in avoiding unnecessary frustration and overcoming the toughest obstacles that are encountered. By using the information that is applicable to your situation and having a better understanding of credit and debt, you can become and remain a debt free citizen. Good Luck!

Contents

CHAPTER 10
BANKRUPTCY: THE LAST RESORT 113

CHAPTER 1

IDENTIFYING A FINANCIAL PROBLEM AND UNDERSTANDING DEBT

CHAPTER 1

IDENTIFYING A FINANCIAL PROBLEM AND UNDERSTANDING DEBT

Getting rid of debt is like getting rid of an illness. First you have to recognize the symptoms and then you have to provide an immediate remedy. If you wait too long before treating the problem, the situation will get worse and it will take longer to recover. If you procrastinate on treating the problem, it may cause long-term pain and discomfort that eventually escalates into a more severe illness which requires a more drastic cure. If the illness progresses too far, it could turn into a chronic condition. Similarly, failure to acknowledge financial problems can escalate into more severe problems that are costly to recover from and require drastic solutions that may damage credit worthiness.

To effectively reduce debt, it is important that you understand how you got into debt. This book will assist you in analyzing your budget and spending habits, but it is equally important to understand how credit works and analyze the way of thinking that led to the irrational spending. To understand why you overspend, you must understand your desires and the impulses that drive them. In our credit society, we are often driven by the illusion that our social status and successes are measured by the amount of goods or services we can consume (buy). Buying discretionary goods allows us to live up to a certain image but often detracts from our "true" wealth. We should measure our success based on the amount of "true" wealth (monetary assets) that we accumulate. "True" wealth is made up of

1

things that we own that can appreciate in value. In other words, if handled correctly, "true" wealth can be used to earn more wealth and provide long-term happiness, security, and prosperity. Irrational spending allows us to portray a wealthy image but detracts from our "true" wealth. Buying discretionary (nonessential) items gives us short-term happiness, but the goods normally depreciate fast and if we do not handle our finances appropriately, their long-term costs may leave us with no "true" wealth to support our image. Eventually, our image may come crashing down.

A common problem for consumers is that due to the nature of credit cards and the relative ease of acquiring unsecured debt (debt that does not involve collateral), we often do not realize there is a problem until we have fallen behind on our accounts. Instead of taking preventative measures to avoid debt problems, consumers often wait too long and react to a problem after it has gotten out of control. We are forced to confront our situation and, from there, we have to fight an uphill battle. Consumers that are the most successful at eliminating debt, adopt a proactive rather than a reactive approach. We have a tendency to assume that things will get better or that good times are here to stay. Alan Greenspan, the Chairman of the Federal Reserve, calls this thinking "irrational exuberance," and even investors who have extra money and play the stock market are guilty of it. You do not have to be delinquent on accounts to have a budgeting problem. As consumers, the simple fact that we can afford minimum monthly payments gives us a false sense of security and does not indicate that we are financially secure. Mismanagement and overuse of credit cards are the biggest dangers that threaten us as consumers, but there are many forms of debt and they can all play a role in "tangling the web." The warning

Hey! You Can't Hide From Your Bill.

2

signs do not always jump out at us because of our natural tendency to continue along the path of pleasure and avoid confronting our difficulties. In other words, when handling our finances, we tend to "take the path of least resistance." We should take a proactive approach and prepare for a worst case scenario but doing so often requires making sacrifices. After all, "ignorance is bliss." To successfully manage finances, it is extremely important that we create a "buffer zone" between relative financial security and financial distress, despite the fact that it may deprive us of some short- term pleasure. The time to start planning is now. All too often, consumers fall delinquent on their financial obligations because unexpected stops in cash flow such as loss of a job, family illness, or sudden short term or long term disability. Many Americans are forced to confront their financial problems when they face life-altering events such as getting married or divorced, having children, or facing unexpected medical bills. To prepare for these events, most financial consultants suggest that consumers should have enough savings to cover 3-6 months in expenses. Don't be a victim of "irrational exuberance," the good times are not always here to stay. Every dollar spent frivolously is a dollar that detracts from your "true" wealth and financial security.

MANAGING YOUR FINANCES LIKE A RESERVOIR

For purposes of helping understand debt, you should think of your financial management as a reservoir. The streams flowing into the reservoir symbolize your household income and the water flowing out of the dam of your reservoir is your discretionary spending. Your normal, necessary, everyday living expenses are paid out of the water in your reservoir and what is left represents your savings and accumulation of wealth (lets call it your pool of wealth). Your goal is to accumulate water (wealth) within your reservoir system, which will indicate that you are in control of your finances as opposed to letting them control you. Irrationally letting too much water (wealth) out of your reservoir system will eventually lead to shortage that creates distress on the system (your finances). It will be easier to pay normal necessary bills if there is a deeper pool of wealth. If an unexpected drought (financial crisis) should occur and you have provided a surplus in your reservoir, you will be equipped to weather the drought until the hard time has passed. If incoming streams flow into and right out of your reservoir system and under the dam, the reservoir will be dry and you will be caught in financial turmoil. The money that is flowing out of the flood gates may be money that you are spending to give the appearance of wealth, but it may just be money sent down the river that leaves your reservoir (savings) dry, leaving you with no true wealth and security.

There are two ways to increase the depth of water in the reservoir. You can increase your income stream or you can be more resistant to the outflow of water (irrational spending). Increasing the income stream is usually much more difficult than building a more resistant dam because it relies, in large part, on factors that are out of your control. If you avoid the reality of a low supply of water or you are waiting for something to happen that will get you out of your situation, you may be "praying for rain" to fill your reservoir. Instead of addressing the root of their problem (budgeting and spending problems), consumers often find themselves doing a desperate "rain dance" and trying to juggle their bills around an income stream that is just not sufficient enough to support their outflow. The key to successfully managing your reservoir is to accumulate water (wealth) behind your dam. Building a stronger dam with better floodgates may be the most effective way of filling your reservoir because controlling the floodgates (spending) is directly within your control. Building your dam may require some sacrifices and some hard work, but the true reward is the pool of (true) wealth that you will find behind your dam. If used wisely, the pool of wealth can appreciate in value and bring more prosperity. It can also give you relative security in times of drought. In order to start building the new dam, you will need to acknowledge that the old reservoir system was flawed and you must accept part of the responsibility for allowing it to be that way.

RECOGNIZING A DEBT PROBLEM

Following are questions that will help determine if you may be in danger of future debt problems:

Do you have savings? Do you find yourself exhausting savings as a way of supporting your debts?

If you do not have savings, you should be concerned because you may not be able to adjust to an unexpected situation that requires additional financial resources. If you are exhausting savings to keep up with your bills, it may be an indication that you are spending more than your income can support.

Do you pay only minimum payments on your credit cards?

If you are only making minimum payments and can afford to pay more, you should. If you can only afford minimum payments or not much more than minimum payments, you are probably overextended and should analyze your budget and adjust your spending behavior. It is likely that if you are thrown into a situation that requires more financial resources, your situation will become unmanageable.

Have you been declined credit or declined a credit line increase?

Being declined for credit is a good sign that you need to evaluate your finances. Creditors use guidelines to determine your credit worthiness and if they decline you, it means that they feel that your finances exhibit signs of trouble.

After you pay your monthly credit card bills, do you accumulate as much or more debt the following month?

This may be a sign that you are dependent on your credit cards to maintain your style of living or supplement day to day living expenses.

Can you account for the total amount of debt that you owe? Do you avoid adding up the total of the amount of your outstanding debt?

If you cannot account for the total amount of debt that you owe, you may be avoiding the problem. You must confront your spending behavior. Stop avoiding the pain of paying on your debt and establish a better repayment plan before the situation becomes unmanageable.

Are your cards nearing or over your available credit limit? Have you ever attempted to make a credit card purchase and had the card declined?

If the answer is yes, it may be another sign that you are turning your cheek to the pain of confronting paying for credit card purchases. It is also a sign that you are not aware of your financial situation. If you were aware of your finances and understood how high your balances were, the situation could have been avoided. Your creditors assign a credit limit to you based on your credit history, outstanding indebtedness, and income. If you are at or near your limit it is a good sign that you are headed for financial trouble.

Are you dependent on cash advances to pay on your other credit obligations?

Danger!!! Stop immediately!! Your income cannot support your style of life. Analyze your budget and make adjustments. You may need to seek outside help for guidance.

Do you purposely hide credit card bills from family members?

Hiding debt from family members is an indication that you realize that there is a problem. The fact that you feel you have to hide your spending behavior from loved ones indicates that you refuse to confront the situation, but realize there is a problem.

Do you float checks or bounce checks?

Floating checks is the practice of issuing a check in hopes that by the time the check is cashed, you will have the money in the account. Floating and/or bouncing checks is an indication that you are living paycheck to paycheck and your finances are in trouble. Floating and bouncing checks indicates that you are not fully aware of your financial situation.

Do you get collection calls from creditors?

Collection calls are a sure sign that you are behind on credit obligations. Don't avoid the problem. Start planning to become current again.

DEBT: GOOD OR EVIL?

In today's credit society, it is nearly impossible to avoid the offers that we receive from banks and credit card companies. The marketing of credit cards is the same as the marketing of products, and credit card companies often tend to play on our ego and emotions. Credit card companies entice us by playing on our "self importance" with flashy high credit line offers on Gold, Platinum, and Titanium cards. The challenge is to ask ourselves if we really need the purchasing power and the temptation that these cards offer.

Behavioral patterns and external influences largely determine the outcome of a debtor's credit experience. To have a positive experience with obtaining debt and maintaining good credit, we must understand and limit the internal and external impulses that drive us. Some people categorize debt as a "necessary evil," which, too a certain extent, may be true. Debt is certainly necessary because most Americans may never be able to make an outright purchase of a new car or home if they could not acquire a line of credit. Some individuals believe that credit worthiness is improved by being completely debt free. However, consumers who have no credit history may be just as likely to be denied for credit as those who have derogatory information on their credit, despite the fact that the person with no credit is completely in control of their finances and the person with credit is not. Lenders are most interested in seeing how consumers handle debt. Having credit allows you to display the history of your finances to lending institutions that are concerned about getting a return on money that they lend. It is important that you establish some form of credit history because credit provides convenience and improves your purchasing power which may improve your quality of life.

Good debt is debt that works for the consumer. Taking a loan on a car is an example of good debt because if you could not obtain a car to get to work in, you probably would not be able to maintain a sufficient income stream to support your family or the style of life that you want. Financing a fancy car that you cannot afford is an example of bad debt because the money that the car allows you to earn is consumed by the car payments. Being "car poor" may ultimately cause you and your family unnecessary distress. A home loan is another example of good debt because homes often appreciate in value and they are usually long-term possessions.

Owning a home may give you a tax break on the interest that you can write off. However, if you purchase too much home, you may put yourself in a situation where the mortgage payments are too high and your financial and emotional freedom is compromised by your mortgage payment. Labeling debt as "good" or "bad' is relative to your ability to comfortably afford payments on the debt without compromising savings and future prosperity.

In today's society, credit may be deemed a necessity in that it is needed to do things like book airfare, rent cars, and purchase items over the Internet. Debt is not an "evil" thing unless we allow it to be, or unless external influences thrust us into a situation in which managing our debt is difficult or impossible. Incurring debt can be "good" because it can help build credit, which may assist you by attaining better interest rates on future purchases and assume more buying power. Debt can be a convenience in emergency situations or when cash is not readily available. Incurring too much debt can hurt your credit and may inhibit you from acquiring the best possible interest rate on future purchases or may even prevent you from acquiring those purchases at all. Excessive debt can place you in a situation in which the debt controls you, instead of you controlling the debt. Severe mismanagement of credit may lead to unforeseen difficulties, which include long-term undue stress levels and feelings of anxiety or depression. Stress caused by excessive debt may have far reaching affects on our relationship with family, friends, and society in general. Studies suggest that over 50 percent of divorces are caused, in part, by financial problems in the household. This poses the question as to whether the debt is the result of the divorce, or the divorce is the result of the stress caused by the debt. Debt problems often escalate to an uncontrollable level when we turn a blind eye to warning signs and hold on to the dream that things will magically get better.

NECESSARY AND DISCRETIONARY SPENDING

When evaluating reasonable use of credit and acquisition of debt, it is important to realize that spending should be categorized into necessary and discretionary spending. Doing so will assist in avoiding situations in which you acquire too much debt relative to the amount of debt that can successfully be supported through your household income. As a means of survival, humans have to provide for their daily necessities such as food, clothing, shelter, and in today's society, even transportation. The cost of providing the basic daily necessities is normally relatively inexpensive and does not create too much drag on our income stream, provided we have not overburdened ourselves with unnecessary debt. There are major discretionary differences in providing necessities for us that pose as threats to our financial well being. There are discretionary choices that we make, regarding the type of food that we choose to eat (or where we like to eat it), the clothes that we choose to wear, the shelter that we call home, and the automobile that we choose for transportation. Choosing to spend too much on simple necessities can bear as much burden on our personal finances as excessive spending on discretionary (nonessential) goods.

Discretionary spending also comes into play when we buy durable goods such as television sets, stereos and CD players, and other household appliances. Due to the fact that these goods are often relatively expensive, consumers often depend on acquiring loans and lines of credit to purchase them. Some of these goods may be considered necessities in today's society but the amount that we spend on them should be limited based on our ability to afford them. Using credit to accumulate durable goods, in combination with irrational spending and repayment behavior, often creates long term financial difficulties. If our personal finances are not relatively secure, we should limit our spending on these items, until our finances become more stable and enable us to afford the "luxury" of purchasing upgraded or fancier models. It is not "bad" or "wrong" to desire goods or services but to successfully avoid the long term strains that they may cause on our finances, it is important that we realize that paying for these goods and services, over time, has a direct impact on our "true" financial stability. In other words, we must realize that our monthly net income drops by the sum of the dollar amounts of every loan or credit card payment that we make each month.

CHAPTER 2

BUDGETING AND COST CUTTING

CHAPTER 2

BUDGETING AND COST CUTTING

In its simplest form, budgeting is comparing income to expenses. There is no better time than now to start recording and evaluating your budget. To be successful at reducing and managing debt, it is extremely important that you create a budget because it allows you to take a "snapshot" of current expenditures, which enables you to analyze spending habits. Taking a "snapshot" allows you to view your finances by looking from the outside in. As consumers, we often tend to generalize when evaluating our spending from the inside out, which causes us to underestimate the cumulative costs of our routine spending behavior. Most consumers have a good knowledge of their income but lose track of their spending because they only account for purchases that were made in the recent past. Our mind's record and perception of our spending habits tends to be inaccurate which prevents us from realizing the effect that spending is having on our "true" income (income minus obligations). We tend to avoid the reality of the long-term effects associated with irrational spending. Budgeting assists in realizing how much our style of living is really costing. It also assists in helping to organize personal finances and realize where to cut back on spending. Creating a budget makes us confront our problems and enables us to establish a starting point in the quest of becoming debt free.

When recording your budget, it is important to use information that is accurate according to your immediate financial situation. Do not "put the cart before the horse" and overestimate your income, because you expect an increase in your household income. If you account for unrealized income, it may cause you to take your budget for granted and underestimate the importance of adjusting spending behavior. An expected income increase is something to be optimistic about, but it should be viewed as a means by which you can decrease your debt, as opposed to viewing it as an additional source of disposable income. On the other hand, if you expect a decrease in household income, plan for it in your budget. By planning for a worse case scenario, you will afford the luxury of being prepared when difficulty arises. If you plan for the worst and the worst never comes, you will end up ahead of the game.

BUDGET WORKSHEET

The following worksheet (Figure 2.1) will help you record and analyze the effects of routine expenditures on your monthly household income. Since most bills are due on a monthly basis, it is best to record your budget on a monthly basis. Start by recording your household income and routine monthly expenditures (bills). The difference between your household income and your routine expenditures represents your disposable income.

BUDGETING: A FRAME OF MIND

Adjusting spending habits after recording a budget is often the most difficult obstacle that you will encounter on your road to debt freedom because it involves making sacrifices through cut backs and changing the style of life that you have grown accustomed to. Let's face it, we are all human and humans are creatures of habit. It may take a while to get adjusted to new spending habits. Many of us grow accustomed to providing immediate gratification to our spending impulses.

When adjusting spending habits, you should not only focus on future spending plans, you should also focus on reducing the current obligations that are causing the financial crunch. The approach that you take to "cutting back" is largely dependent on your likes and dislikes and the point you are at in your life. Your approach should depend largely on the time frame that is set as your goal for getting out of debt. Choose a target date by which you expect to reach your

Figure 2.1   Budgeting Worksheet

MONTHLY NET INCOME (AFTER-TAXES)

1ST INCOME	$_____
2ND INCOME	$_____
BONUSES & PROFIT SHARING	$_____
ALIMONY & CHILD SUPPORT	$_____
OTHER INCOME	$_____
TOTAL INCOME	**$_____**

ROUTINE MONTHLY EXPENSES

MORTGAGE / RENTAL PAYMENT	$_____
GROCERY / PET SUPPLIES / TOLIETRIES	$_____
HOME / CELL PHONE	$_____
ELECTRIC / GAS BILL	$_____
CABLE BILL	$_____
WATER BILL	$_____
HOMEOWNER / RENTERS INSURANCE	$_____
AUTO / LIFE INSURANCE	$_____
AUTOMOTIVE REPAIRS	$_____
FUEL / TRANSPORTATION EXPENSE	$_____
CLOTHING	$_____
LAUNDRY / DRY CLEANING	$_____
ENTERTAINMENT/VACATION	$_____
CHILD CARE	$_____
ALIMONY / CHILD SUPPORT	$_____
MEDICAL / DENTAL EXPENSE	$_____
EDUCATIONAL / SCHOOL EXPENSE	$_____
HOLIDAY / GIFT SPENDING	$_____
LAWN CARE / SUPPLIES	$_____
PERSONAL GROOMING / HAIRCUTS	$_____
TOTAL EXPENSE	**$**

Figure 2.1 Budgeting Worksheet (continued)

MONTHLY CREDIT CARD AND LOAN EXPENSES

CREDIT CARDS

NAME	INTEREST RATE	PAYMENT
1. _____	_____ %	$_____
2. _____	_____ %	$_____
3. _____	_____ %	$_____
4. _____	_____ %	$_____
5. _____	_____ %	$_____
6. _____	_____ %	$_____
7. _____	_____ %	$_____
8. _____	_____ %	$_____
9. _____	_____ %	$_____
10._____	_____ %	$_____

LOANS

1. AUTO LOAN / LEASE #1	_____ %	$_____
2. AUTO LOAN / LEASE #2	_____ %	$_____
3. 1ST MORTGAGE	_____ %	$_____
4. 2ND MORTGAGE	_____ %	$_____
5. 3RD MORTGAGE	_____ %	$_____
6. PERSONAL LOANS #1	_____ %	$_____
7. PERSONAL LOAN #2	_____ %	$_____
8. PERSONAL LOAN #3	_____ %	$_____
9. STUDENT LOAN #1	_____ %	$_____
10.STUDENT LOAN #2	_____ %	$_____

TOTAL LOAN / CREDIT CARD PAYMENTS $_____

TOTAL MONTHLY NET INCOME	$ _____
TOTAL ROUTINE MONTHLY EXPENSES	$- _____
TOTAL LOAN / CREDIT CARD PAYMENTS	$- _____

TOTAL DISPOSABLE INCOME $= _____

goal. It should be reasonable as compared to your willingness to sacrifice. If you are tolerant to sudden and drastic changes, you can make drastic cut backs that will enable you to get back on your feet and ahead of the game quickly. The ability to endure drastic changes is often dependent on your threshold to the pain that will be cause by the sacrifices that will be made. If you own a home, you can sell the home and move in with family or move to a home or apartment that is less of a drag on your budget, but making drastic changes is not agreeable to every one. If you have extra room in your home, you could take in a roommate and collect rent to increase your income stream. If you determine that your car payment is too high, you can sell the car and purchase a less expensive model or purchase a used car (doing so often helps you reduce your insurance costs). You can temporarily eliminate vacations and weekend travel. You can even obtain a second job to supplement your income.

Taking sudden measures to reduce debt is a very effective option, but it is not an option for most consumers. Families may be restricted in their ability to make drastic sacrifices. When adjusting spending habits, it may be necessary for the whole family to make sacrifices. Getting rid of a car or home or renting to a housemate is usually not an option for a family. Obtaining a second job may be an option, but many consumers cannot adjust to such drastic measures without satisfying their desire to spend quality time with their family. Taking a "cold turkey" approach to reducing debt will get you to your goal the quickest, but the sacrifice that is required may cause you to lose sight of your goals. Most consumers adopt a more gradual, progressive approach to limiting their expenditures, but they should focus on cutting back as much as possible. By adopting a gradual approach, it will take more time to reach your goal, but it will be easier to adjust to and adhere to your spending and savings plan because the sacrifices are not as hard felt. A more gradual approach is usually more conducive to consumers who have a family or want debt reduction to be less evident to their peers.

KEEPING YOUR GOALS IN SIGHT

At some time you will have the desire to return to your old spending habits, but remember that doing so works against your ultimate goal of getting out of debt. Getting off track will cause you to wait longer before realizing your goal. When adjusting your spending habits, it is important you allow for some "leisure money" in your new budget. The purpose of budgeting is to trim expenditures back to a more reasonable level, not to take all of the joy out of living. As you pay your bills off, you will experience progressive stages of success (maybe bringing yourself current or paying off a credit card). As you experience success, it may encourage and motivate you to work harder at becoming debt free. However, if you celebrate too much with success, it may create a false feeling that you are completely in control again and you may lose sight of your goal. When you achieve some success at reducing your debt, it is okay to rejoice (you deserve it) but it is important that you do not lose sight of your goal. It may be helpful to post reminders in places where you will constantly be reminded of your goal of becoming debt free. You can cut out pictures of images that are symbolic of your goals and the people that will benefit from reaching those goals. Post them as reminders of the rewards that will be available when your goals are met. Maybe post a picture of a house, a picture symbolizing retirement, or a picture of your family. Keep changing pictures if you have many goals. It's up to you—posting reminders will help to prioritize and keep your goals in sight (literally).

The Three Pronged Approach: Accelerating Payments, Adjusting Spending Habits, and Cost Cutting

18

Adjusting Your Repayment Behavior

Adjusting your spending behavior and finding less costly alternatives will enable you to minimize expenditures and increase the amount of your disposable income. Disposable income should not be viewed as income that is truly "disposable" for purposes of discretionary spending. Instead, it should be used to reduce the long-term costs of interest that accumulates on credit obligations. With more disposable income you will be able to take a more aggressive approach to reducing debt. A very effective method of paying down debt is to focus more of your disposable income towards "accelerating" payment on your outstanding obligations. When accelerating payments on your debt, target the accounts with the highest interest rate. You can record the interest rates on the budget worksheet (Figure 2.1) near each of your obligations. After meeting the monthly payment requirements on all of your regular debts (account for minimum payments on your credit cards), allocate as much of your disposable income as possible to pay extra on the highest interest rate accounts. Special consideration should be given to credit cards because interest usually compounds faster on "revolving" debt. By targeting the highest interest rate account, the balance on which the high rate of interest can accrue will decrease faster and you will get "more bang for the buck" than if you spread the extra money out equally among all of your monthly payment obligations. When you pay an account off, take the monthly payment that you were allocating toward that account and apply it to the next highest interest rate account.

The following chart (Figure 2.2) demonstrates how interest rates will determine the cost of borrowing and the approximate payoff time on a credit card with a balance of $4,500. The example assumes that the debtor is paying minimum payments of 2% of their monthly balance.

19

Figure 2.2   INTEREST MATTERS

CREDIT CARD	INTEREST RATE	TOTAL INTEREST PAID	MONTHS TO PAYOFF
CREDIT CARD #1	12.5%	$1,922	72 Months
CREDIT CARD #2	16.5%	$3,216	86 Months
CREDIT CARD #3	20.5%	$5,814	115 Months

COST CUTTING IDEAS

When you have finished recording your budget, try to minimize the cost of regular monthly expenses. Minimizing costs will maximize your disposable income with which to accelerate payment on debts. Following are examples of regular monthly expenses and suggestions on how to reduce their effect on your disposable income.

Reduce Routine Expenditures

Food- Use coupons or take advantage of store sales. Use a grocery store discount card if the store offers one. Make price comparisons from store to store but remember to stick to the list of necessities that you created before going shopping. Don't be enticed by sales on discretionary items that you do not need. You may be able to benefit by purchasing items in bulk stores, especially if you have to provide for a family. Be careful, bulk purchasing is not always the most cost effective, so shop the prices. Nonperishable items can be purchased in bulk and stored in your pantry or freezer. Don't be afraid to buy while the buying is good as long as you know that you have enough storage room and will eventually use the food. Bulk purchasing is especially effective with canned and nonperishable goods. Cut back on the number of times that you eat out. "Brown bag" lunches are an option for the serious cost cutter. Although frozen meals and snacks are very convenient, they are expensive because of the high costs of packaging and distribution.

Clothes- Search for end of season markdowns and irregulars that have imperfections that are not noticeable. "Hand me downs" are a great way of cutting costs on children's clothes. Outlet shopping may be cheaper, but price shop them carefully because prices are not always lower at outlets.

Phone- Limit unnecessary long distance calls. Look for a long distance provider that offers you the most favorable rate. If family members are overusing the phone, create guidelines concerning phone use. Often, long distance providers will give better rates on certain days of the week. *Example: If your provider offers 10 cent Sundays, limit your long distance calls to Sundays, if possible.* Pit the long distance providers against each other and do competitive rate comparisons. Carriers often engage in "rate wars" that you might be able to take advantage of.

Cable Bill- Analyze your cable package. Do you really need all of the channels that you are paying for, or can you downgrade to a cheaper cable package? Can you do without cable TV? Remember, the more television you watch, the more temptation you will face from marketing and advertisements.

Laundry/cleaning- Look for the cheapest dry cleaning service. Many dry cleaners will handle any item for only 1$. When doing laundry, try to only wash full loads. You will save money, on the water and electric bill and on detergent. If you do not have a washer and dryer, consider paying for your laundry by the pound instead of using coin-op machines. It may be cheaper and you won't have to do the laundry yourself or pay for detergent or laundry products. Buying laundry detergent in bulk will save money.

Vacation- Everybody needs a break but taking a vacation does not mean that you have to take a break from cost cutting. Analyze your entertainment and vacation expenses. Avoid paying long term for a vacation that only lasts for a relatively short period of time. Try to travel to somewhere cheaper or closer that still gives the same desired "get away" that you need. Travel clubs and web sites often offer favorable discounts on hotel and air fare. It may be worth joining one if you travel a lot. Take advantage of hotel promotions. It is best to travel during off-peak times of the year or during weekdays when flights are cheaper. You can make your vacation a budgeting goal by setting aside a portion of every paycheck until the vacation is paid for. Bring snacks and lunches while you travel to cut down on food stops. If you are in another country, know the exchange rate so you do not pay more than you think on purchases. If you do a lot of domestic travel, state welcome centers offer travel brochures that include lodging and food discounts.

Books, Newspapers, Subscriptions- Analyze incoming mail. Are you paying for periodicals that you no longer read or utilize? Watch out for passive prescription practices through which magazines are sent and you are billed, despite the fact that you never wanted or requested them. Some magazines employ automatic renewal practices. If you no longer want to subscribe to a magazine, call to cancel when it is up for renewal. Try to avoid being enticed by newspaper flyers, magazine advertisements or mail order catalogs.

Medical Insurance- Double check to be sure you are not footing the bill for an expense that the Health Care Provider should be covering. When in doubt, appeal a denial on health care coverage. Be proactive, preventative medicine may save a lot of money in the long run.

Drugs and Medical Supplies- Buy generic drugs. Buy over the counter medicines. If your employer offers a flexible spending account or "cafeteria plan," take advantage of it because you can pay for health care costs out of pre-tax income. Preventative health measures can save a lot of money in the long run.

Auto Loans- If you are behind on your automobile loan, contact the company that finances the loan. Inquire about doing an auto loan extension. Usually they will make you pay the interest, only, on the monthly payments that you want to defer and they will tack the payments on to the end of the loan. Most car loan finance companies will allow you to "extend" up to three payments at one time, but will only allow you to extend payment a limited number of times. Taking an extension can help you to become current again and avoid costly late fees and damage to your credit. *Unfortunately, extensions are not usually an option on car leases.*

Evaluate Mortgage Insurance- If you have 20% equity in your home, you are no longer required to carry Mortgage Insurance Protection (MIP) on the house. In most cases, the premium for Mortgage Insurance Protection is built into the escrow portion of your mortgage payment. If you have 20% equity in your home, you can contact the mortgage lender to have the MIP removed. This will help you reduce the mortgage payment.

> *IF YOU HAVE A FHA LOAN, YOU WILL NOT BE ALLOWED TO REMOVE THE MIP, EVEN IF YOU HAVE 20% EQUITY IN THE HOME.

Pay Your Own Insurance and Property Tax Bills-The escrow portion of your mortgage payment covers the mortgage insurance and tax bills. If you request that the mortgage company eliminate your escrow, you can take the funds that normally would have paid to the escrow on the mortgage and earn interest on them. Simply deposit them in a money market account, bank CD, bond, or T-Bill that matures when the funds are due. You will have gained by earning a return on the money that would normally have just stayed in an escrow account.

> * IT IS VERY IMPORTANT TO DEPOSIT THE FUNDS IN AN INVESTMENT TO INSURE THAT THE FUNDS ARE AVAILABLE WHEN THE TAX AND INSURANCE BILLS ARE DUE. AVOID USING THE FUNDS TO MAKE DISCRETIONARY PURCHASES, PAY ROUTINE LIVING EXPENSES, OR MAKE AN INVESTMENT THAT DOES NOT GIVE YOU A GUARANTEED RATE OF RETURN.

Make Adjustments in Tax Exemptions- If you receive a tax refund every year, consider increasing the number of exemptions on your W4 tax form. Increasing exemptions will enable you to get more money in your paycheck during the course of the year. This will enable you to accelerate payment on any high interest bills that you owe. If you do not have high interest bills, direct the extra money to a 401k retirement plan, use it as an IRA contribution, or accelerate payment on your mortgage or any other bills you may have.

> *IF YOU ADJUST EXEMPTIONS HIGHER, CHANCES ARE, YOU WILL OWE A LARGER TAX BILL AT THE END OF THE TAX YEAR. BE SURE TO PROVIDE FOR MONEY TO PAY THE TAXES BEFORE THE DUE DATE OR THE IRS WILL CHARGE PENALTIES AND HIGH INTEREST ON YOUR DELINQUENT TAXES. CONSULT YOUR TAX ADVISOR.

Avoid Bank and ATM Surcharges- It is estimated that the average amount of bank transaction fees paid per year by a consumer is $250. Normally, you will be charged an ATM fee if the machine from which you are withdrawing money is not a sponsoring bank. You may be charged a fee by the bank that sponsors the machine and also from your own bank. To significantly cut back on this expense, adjust your use of ATM machines. Try to set a weekly budget and take enough money out of your account each week to meet that budget. By doing so, you will limit the number of ATM transactions and reduce the fees that you pay to the bank. It may be wise to switch to a bank that has many ATMs in your area or switch to a bank that is very close to work or home. By doing so, you will have access to money without paying fees. Avoid transaction fees by using ATM cards at supermarkets, because many markets let you take cash out without incurring fees. Some service station convenient stores actively promote "no service fee" ATM machines. Every dollar counts.

Saving on Auto Insurance

Personal Automobile Insurance Premium is based on the "risk" associated with providing coverage for a given individual or group of individuals (family). Once the risk factor has been determined, the insurance provider applies a given premium or price that is assigned to the risk of insuring the individual or group. The premium is determined by comparing the risk involved with insuring the policy holder(s), to the prior loss experienced for insuring similar policyholders. To determine the risk, the insurance company takes different factors into account, such as age, past driving history, type of vehicle, marital status, how far the policy holder drives to work, and the area where the vehicle is principally driven or garaged.

Following are rating factors and what you can do about them to save money on your insurance premium:

Number of drivers in the household- Make sure that the policy covers only drivers that are in your household and use your vehicles. If you do not keep the insurance company updated, they may continue to rate for drivers that have moved out of the household or that have their own insurance policies. Most insurance companies will not allow you to remove a child who is in college. They consider the child to still be in the household and at risk of driving the vehicle. Many insurance companies offer a "college away" discount to adjust premium for family members who are away at college and do not use the vehicles as much.

Distance driven to work- Be sure that your insurance company has the correct information on the miles that are driven per year and the miles that are driven to and from work. Rates are determined, in part, by the length of the commute and how often you drive.

Discounts- Most insurance companies offer discounts for different qualifications. Some common discounts are Safe Driver Discounts, Multi-Policy Discounts (if you have both home and auto insurance through the same carrier), Security Alarm Discount, Good Student Discount, Student Away Discount, Superior Driver Discount, etc. Contact your insurance provider to make sure the policy is rated correctly based on discounts that you may be eligible for.

Garaging Information- Insurance providers often rate based on garaging information. If a car is parked on the street, it may carry a higher premium than if it is parked in a garage or in a private driveway. Contact the insurance provider to make sure they have the correct parking information for your vehicle.

Driving Record- All insurance companies rate based on driving records. If you obtained insurance when you had accidents or traffic violations, you may have been placed with a nonstandard insurance carrier. Nonstandard insurance coverage usually costs more because it is coverage that is considered higher risk. When applying for insurance, most companies account for accident and traffic violations that occurred within the three-year period prior to the application date. You may still be paying a higher rate despite the fact that the violations and accidents are off your record. If you have a clean driving record (accident and violation free) within the last three years and you are with a nonstandard or assigned risk policy, it would be wise to shop the insurance around to find a more favorable rate.

Type of Vehicle- Insurance premiums are rated according to the type of vehicle that is being insured. Classic, Luxury, Specialty, and High Performance vehicles can drive auto premiums up considerably. When purchasing a new vehicle, review all of the "assumed" costs involved with insuring the vehicle. These costs can often be unrealized and may increase your monthly expenditures considerably. If you have any concern about how a vehicle may effect your premium, contact your insurance company or agent and get a free "hypothetical" quote to determine how the new vehicle may effect the premium.

Compare Rates

Don't assume that the insurance company is giving you the best rate. Rating factors differ from insurance company to insurance company and premiums often vary drastically. Your driving record may have improved significantly since you last acquired coverage so you may be due for a rate decrease.

How to shop around for the best rate:

• Find the "declarations page" for your current insurance policy. The declaration is a summary of your policy limits, coverage, and the amount you are paying for insurance coverage. The declarations page will also reflect the time period during which coverage exists. Some policies renew every six months while others renew every year, so compare coverage premiums based on billing periods of equal length.

• Once you have the declarations page and know your coverage, **GET QUOTES** on policies from other insurance companies. Look in the yellow pages for insurance companies or agencies that provide coverage in your local area. Insurance companies and agents will give rate quotes for free, so shop around as much as possible. Independent agents are good sources for insurance quotes because they write policies for several different insurance companies and can do the shopping for you. They will not charge for placing coverage through an insurance company. It is best to do some shopping on your own to see if you can beat the rates that the independent agent has quoted. Independent agents often write policies for only a select group of insurance companies. Another good source for automobile insurance quotes is Internet sites such as www.Insweb.com. The more quotes obtained, the more likely it is that you will find the cheapest possible rate.

Adjusting Insurance Coverage

You can often reduce the insurance premium that you are paying by altering the terms of your insurance policy. Following are some suggestions on what coverage changes can be made:

Increasing or Decreasing Deductibles- Adjusting the deductible will allow you to have more control over the insurance premium that you pay. The insurance deductible is the amount of money that you are responsible for covering in the event of an accident or claim. The deductible applies to physical damage coverage only (comprehensive and collision coverage).

EXAMPLE: IF YOU HAVE A $500 DEDUCTIBLE AND GOT INTO AN ACCIDENT IN WHICH THE DEDUCTIBLE WAS APPLICABLE, YOU WOULD BE RESPONSIBLE FOR COVERING THE FIRST $500 OF DAMAGE AND THE INSURANCE COMPANY WOULD BE RESPONSIBLE FOR THE REMAINDER.

By increasing the deductible, you accept more of the financial burden and will have to pay more in the event of an accident before the insurer picks up coverage. Your policy premium will be lower because you are accepting more of the responsibility of paying for damage in the event of an accident. If you decrease your deductible, you are asking the insurance company to cover more of the risk of an accident so the policy premium will be higher.

Eliminate Physical Damage Coverage- If you have an older vehicle, you can consider eliminating the physical damage coverage. If the vehicle is not paid off and the bank still holds the title, they may not allow you to drop physical damage coverage. If you drop the insurance, they can apply insurance, which you would be responsible for paying (sometimes at a very high premium). However, if you have an older vehicle that is paid off and you are not concerned about any physical damage that may occur to the vehicle, consider dropping physical damage coverage (comprehensive and collision coverage) because it will reduce the premium.

Eliminate Bad Driving Risks- Since insurance premiums are based on the loss experience associated with insuring certain risks, it is sometimes cost effective to remove bad risks from your policy.

PROBLEM: YOUR CHILD HAS A BAD DRIVING RECORD AND HE/SHE IS ON YOUR AUTOMOBILE POLICY. HE/SHE MAY BE DRIVING THE INSURANCE PREMIUM A LOT HIGHER BECAUSE HE/SHE INCREASES THE CHANCE OF AN ACCIDENT OR A CLAIM IN ONE OF YOUR VEHICLES.

SOLUTION: PLACE HIM/HER ON A SEPARATE INSURANCE POLICY WITH THEIR VEHICLE. BY "SPINNING THEM OFF" TO THEIR OWN POLICY, YOU WILL SEPARATE THE RISK FROM YOUR POLICY. THIS SHOULD REDUCE THE OVERALL PREMIUM FOR COVERING YOUR FAMILY.

Controlling Holiday Spending

The following holiday spending ideas can limit the expense of holiday shopping:

⇨Establish a budget in advance. Determine how much money to allocate towards holiday gifts and then decide who to purchase gifts for. This will give you an idea as to how much you are willing to spend on each individual gift. It may help to look at previous holiday bills. Include food, decorations, and travel in your holiday budget. It is helpful to establish a holiday spending account in advance and allocate funds to the account out of every paycheck leading up to the holiday.

⇨Avoid buying on credit if possible. Try to make it through the holidays on a cash and carry basis. If you do use credit, use the card with the lowest interest rate and try, as hard as possible, to pay off the balance when you receive your billing statement.

⇨Instead of buying many gifts, pick a name out of a hat. Set a price limit on the gift. Not only will this save you money, it will help to avoid the hassle of having to shop for many different people with many different tastes. By giving gifts this way everybody is satisfied and expenditures and hassle are limited. This approach allows you to focus on one individual and getting them the best possible gift. Grab bag gift giving is another good money saving idea that eliminates hassle and expense.

⇨Shop around. Don't assume that every store offers the same price. Be price conscious and look for sales. Try browsing the Internet. On-line shopping may offer advantages in price and convenience. If possible arrange gift exchange with relatives or friends after the holidays to take advantage of post holiday sales and store inventory liquidation.

▷It's the thought that counts. As opposed to making material offerings, provide a service which has it's own inherent value. Sometimes services are the best gifts to give because their value is appreciated when their need arises. Services to offer are baby-sitting, lawn or garden care, transportation, pet care, car washing, cleaning and maintenance, housekeeping and house cleaning, snow removal, etc. The value of services is apparent long after material gifts have lost their appeal.

CHAPTER 3

UNDERSTANDING IMPULSE BUYING
AND ADDRESSING SPENDING HABITS

CHAPTER 3

UNDERSTANDING IMPULSE BUYING AND ADDRESSING SPENDING HABITS

DEFEATING EXTERNAL INFLUENCES

In today's society, we are continuously tempted with advertising and marketing schemes. Every time we turn on our television, get on the Internet, or page through our favorite magazine, we are offered emotional images that many of us feel we have to live up to as means of fulfilling a successful image. Advertisers go so far as to suggest that if we do not purchase certain brands or logos, we will not be able to achieve our desired "human potential" or social status. Most consumers are victims of credit abuse only if they allow themselves to be. Commercialism causes consumers to victimize themselves through lack of self-control and feeds their competitive instincts. Advertisements distort our perceptions and create irrational needs such as the need to "Keep up with the Jones" that results from our desire to outdo our peers. In the scheme of things, the advertisers are the predators and we are the prey. To successfully get out of debt, we should take measures to remove ourselves from the danger of being preyed upon.

Advertisements are often manipulative, misleading, and deceitful in that they have a vested interest in enticing us to purchase the goods that they are marketing us. Marketers understand that products may not appeal to our true needs so they have to create false needs by creating images that prey on our senses and emotions and "implant" our desire to purchase their products. When we are enticed to make purchases based on our emotions, we often fall into the most destructive spending behavior, impulse buying. We are conditioned to believe that accumulation of possessions is the true standard in evaluating our importance and success and that the standard is judged by how much we spend, rather than how much we can save.

To be successful at changing our spending behavior, we have to challenge the marketing game or limit our exposure to it. It is a game that is played on the marketer's field because we are surrounded by their constant tempting messages and it is nearly impossible to avoid them. Retail stores and supermarket chains hire outside consulting firms who specialize in consumer spending psychology. Their job is to arrange the goods that are offered in the store so as to create the greatest impulse to buy. Retailers often place their most expensive merchandise at the front of their stores because they realize that consumers will use their senses to "test the goods out", which will create an emotional link or desire for their products. To be successful at debt reduction, we must beat the marketers at their own game and realize the difference between our "emotional" needs and our "actual" needs. If we do not evaluate our spending behaviors, the challenge of decreasing our debt will continue to clash with the artificially stimulated desire to buy on impulse and we will continue to fall prey to the marketers and advertisers. As you build your road to debt freedom, it is extremely important that you avoid the urge of impulse buying. If we continue to succumb to our buying "impulses," we will undermine our true, self-created, personal goal of getting out of debt and we may even fall further into debt. Additionally, we will be letting the marketer's and advertiser's programmed impulses destroy our dreams of prosperity and security, while they fulfill their own goal of making money.

AVOIDING TEMPTATION

An effective way to limit spending is to decrease the exposure to the stimuli that create our false need (impulse) for discretionary products and services. Following are measures that you can take to reduce your exposure to artificially created impulses:

- Reduce your exposure to television commercials and home shopping programs

- Do not become consumed by Internet retail sites
- Limit your exposure to magazine advertising or mail order catalogs
- Do not go shopping out of boredom or as a means of providing entertainment, shop with a purpose
- Limit exposure to individuals who exhibit spending behavior that you are trying to avoid
- Limit exposure to individuals who are critical of your desire to get out of debt

Have you noticed?

⇨ Impulse items such as candy, magazines and knick-knack items are strategically sold at the check out counter where monetary transactions are conducted.

⇨ Necessities such as milk, eggs, and bread are strategically placed at the back corner of the store opposite the entrance so consumers must walk past all of the discretionary goods that they do not necessarily need.

⇨ Bakeries and delicatessens are often placed in the front of stores to entice the consumers with pleasant smells and sites.

⇨ Department stores place elaborately decorated fragrance counters at the entrance of stores to attract customers to the tempting smells and sites.

⇨ Electronics stores place their large "testable" merchandise at the front of the store while items that are necessary to make them work such as accessories, batteries, and parts are placed in the back. This causes the consumer to focus on their "desire" for the merchandise and fail to realize the other cost of enabling them to work.

⇨ Car dealers are often insistent that you test drive a vehicle before they talk any further to you.

THE INTERNAL STRUGGLE: FIGHTING THE PLEASURE-PAIN DILEMMA

To make successfully adaptations to your spending behavior, you must realize the "true" value of money. Your mind's conception of the value of a dollar should not change simply because the dollar is not in your hand. Often, individuals who are experiencing debt problems exhibit irrational spending behavior because they lose the concept of the value of money at the time of a purchase. However, they are forced to face the costs of prolonged repayment in the long term.

We are only human and it is a natural human instinct to avoid pain and seek immediate pleasure. Credit cards have contributed immensely to irrational consumer spending because they capitalize on the pleasure-pain principal and make purchasing discretionary items relatively pain free in the short term. The pain free purchasing power of credit cards and their convenience, combined with our false needs that are created by marketing and advertising temptations, make it very difficult for us to refrain from impulse buying. We are more inclined to make impulsive purchases with credit cards. Unlike making cash purchases, we do not have to physically part with our money. Cash transactions involve a physical separation from our money, which helps us to understand that our financial resources are limited and evaluate the importance of each and every one of our discretionary purchases. However, when using credit cards, we can disassociate the painful realization that a purchase is decreasing or exceeding the amount of our disposable income. To complicate matters, our credit cards allow us to procrastinate and diminish the pain of our purchases by allowing us to make minimum monthly payments. To further complicate matters, credit card users can simply write a check to pay for purchases which completely removes paper money from the process of discretionary spending. It is important that consumers understand that credit cards do not actually pay for purchases. They simply transfer the money that is owed on the purchases to another party that charges interest for providing the privilege of allowing the consumer to pay for the purchase over time. Often, procrastinating by making minimum monthly payments leads to a situation in which we continue to spend to the point where even our minimum monthly payment is unaffordable or stressful on our budget. At this point, all of the pain that we have "brushed under the carpet" can crash down all at once.

USING DEBIT CARDS

Debit cards are effective for consumers because they provide the convenience of electronically deducting purchases directly from their checking account. This process removes the hassle of writing a check, presenting identification and providing personal information. Debit cards are linked directly to the consumer's checking account and the full amount of each purchase will be deducted directly from the account. Depending on the kind of debit card a consumer uses, the funds will be deducted from the account within three business days of the day on which a purchase is made. Some debit cards are "on line" and take the funds out of an account at the time of the purchase and others take a few days to "clear" the account, much like a personal check. Utilizing a debit card is an effective way of dealing with impulse buying because it enables consumers to pay immediately for purchases that are made with the card. Paying immediately defeats the bad habit of procrastinating on repayment, which enables consumers to avoid the cumulative high interest charges associated with borrowing from credit cards.

Consumers must pay careful attention to keeping track of the purchases that they make when using a debit card. If used recklessly, a debit card can leave a consumer with no money with which to pay routine expenditures or provide the bare living essentials because it can drain the money in their checking account. Since debit cards deduct funds directly from their checking account, consumers must pay careful attention to balancing their checkbook and keeping track of the outstanding checks and debit card charges. Debit cards provide all of the short-term conveniences of credit cards without offering the temptation that leads to long term overextension of finances.

TAKING THE "IMPULSE" OUT OF BUYING

The following guidelines will help you limit purchasing temptation:

- Before shopping, look through sales flyers to determine which stores will offer necessity goods for the cheapest price. If necessary, shop at more than one store to take advantage of the best possible prices.
- Create a target list before your shop. Try to limit your list to necessity items.
- Set a predetermined spending limit for each shopping trip. Determine how much you can spend based on your budget.
- Don't be lured by sales on discretionary items or store credit cards that offer percentage discounts on purchases. Store card solicitations are enticing and they make it very easy to spend

impulsively. Often, the discount that store cards provide is overcome by the high interest that you will pay on the purchases that you make.

- Avoid face to face sample counters. They encourage us to use our senses to look, feel, smell, taste, and hear, which often contributes to irrational spending behavior. Sales representatives are often very good at using guilt or pressure to lure consumers into making purchases.
- Leave your credit cards and checkbook at home.
- Replace credit cards with a debit card
- Don't just shop to shop. Have a target list and abide by it. Window- shopping is very tempting but dangerous. Try to avoid shopping as a form of entertainment.
- If you use credit cards, wrap them in a dollar so when you go to use them, you are reminded about the "true" value of money.
- If there is an urge to buy an item that is not a necessity, walk away. Sleep on it. If it means that much to you, it will be worth going back for the next day. Chances are, you won't go back for it.

CONTROLLING DISCRETIONARY SPENDING

Create Spending Guidelines and Substitutes for Expensive Habits

After you are finished recording and analyzing your income and routine expenditures, you should evaluate your discretionary spending. Do not try to account for the past month's purchases because it is nearly impossible to remember all of your discretionary purchases. Start immediately, keep records of each and every one of the purchases that you make on a daily basis. After one month of record keeping, you will realize the cumulative effect that your discretionary spending habits are having on your disposable income.

Putting a limit on expensive habits is an effective way of managing your spending. Cutting back is a very important part of saving money, but it should not require that you take all of the fun out of your life. Creating a set of guidelines to govern discretionary spending will limit unnecessary spending and help you save money. If you go to the movies five times per month, you can create a guideline that limits trips to the theater to just two times per month. Creating a set of guidelines is even more successful and easier to adhere to when combined with substituting for costly discretionary spending habits. The sacrifice that you make by cutting back can be made easier by substituting expensive spending habits with less cost costly alternatives that offer nearly the same amount of personal satisfaction. Using the movie example, an alternative that you could use is renting movies instead of going to the theater. If you have a family you will not have to purchase multiple tickets, your only expense will be the movie rental. Not only will you save money by not paying for movie tickets, you will also save by not buying movie treats such as popcorn, soda, and candy. The sacrifices that you make are temporary, and when you reach your financial goal and feel as though your finances are more stable, you can readjust your budget to allow for more discretionary spending.

Following are areas where you may be concentrating discretionary spending and where you can create guidelines and look for less expensive alternatives:

Sports- Some sports create a major drag on your budget because the equipment or "court time" that they require is very expensive. A good temporary substitute may be a sport that is relatively inexpensive but equally enjoyable. Many outdoor activities are relatively cost free. YMCA's or YWCA's are much more affordable than private health clubs. Other possible alternatives are community pools and involvement in recreation department activities.

Hobbies- Some hobbies tend to be very expensive because they involve collecting "rare" or "authentic" merchandise. Membership in hobby clubs can be expensive but admission at hobby and craft shows is usually free or relatively cheap. Attending craft and hobby shows allows troubled consumers to continue their enthusiasm for their interests and may even serve as encouragement to attain their goal of becoming debt free so they can pursue their interest more. However, hobby and craft enthusiasts must control discretionary spending at hobby and craft shows.

Entertainment- Evaluate the cumulative costs of expensive entertainment (sporting events, movies and plays, bars and night clubs, rock concerts, theme parks, travel). Look for less expensive forms of entertainment. Possible alternatives include going to local or state parks, museums, free concerts, and libraries.

Snacking and Dining Out- Try to make dining out a treat instead of a regular occurrence. Try to limit the number of occasions that you dine out. Assign one night of each week to dine out (maybe Friday). This will give you and the family something to look forward to. When going out to eat, look for reasonably priced restaurants. In many communities, entertainment books are offered that give discounts on local restaurants. Dining out for lunch is convenient but expensive, so try to set a weekly limit. If you live close to work, you can go home for lunch. If not, you may be able to bring lunch to work. Bringing snacks to work can help avoid purchasing from vending machines and snack stands.

Vices (Cigarettes/Alcohol)- Try to limit or stop habits that may be hazardous to your health. Vices are usually very expensive because they are subject to very high taxes. Depending on where you live, if you smoke one pack of cigarettes per day it can cost anywhere from $900 to $1500 per year.

Music (Tapes/Compact Disks)- Compile your favorite songs by recording them on one tape. Music tends to be trendy. How many times have you purchased a tape or disk, listened to it, and then grown tired of it? How many tapes or disks have you purchased only to listen to one particular song? If you borrow a disk or tape from a friend and do not grow tired of it, it may be worth buying.

Questions to ask yourself?

⇨Do I really need it?

⇨If I buy it, will I be compromising my priorities in life?

⇨Will I be unhappy if I don't buy it?

⇨Am I buying it to fulfill my needs or am I buying it to fulfill an image?

⇨Is there a less expensive alternative that will satisfy me nearly as much?

⇨Have I shopped around for this product elsewhere?

⇨Will I grow tired of it?

⇨Am I paying more for quality or just for a designer or brand name?

CHAPTER 4

CREDIT CARDS:
UNDERSTANDING THE INNER WORKINGS

CHAPTER 4

CREDIT CARDS: UNDERSTANDING THE INNER WORKINGS

To successfully manage your finances, it is extremely important that when you are shopping for a credit card, you treat it like a normal purchase. Always shop around for the credit offer that best economically accommodates you as a credit user. Research the terms of use on the credit card by asking specific questions or by reading the cardholder agreement. Before choosing a card you need to understand how the credit card works. If used wisely, there are many benefits to having credit cards. They can help build credit, which can help you realize lifelong dreams, such as purchasing a home. Credit cards can be very useful when dealing with emergency situations in which you do not have cash. Credit cards are necessary if there is a need to book a hotel room, rent a car, book a flight, or cash a check. To maximize the benefits of credit cards, you must fully understand how they work and adjust your use accordingly.

UNDERSTANDING INTEREST RATES

Credit cards are not offered merely as a convenience to a consumer. The primary reason for their existence is to generate revenue for the financial institutions that issue them. Credit card companies are required to post interest rates in terms of an Annual Percentage Rate (APR). The APR that credit cards offer varies greatly and as a smart consumer, your main concern should be obtaining a card with the lowest possible effective rate of interest. There are laws, which vary state to state, that govern limits on interest and fees that credit card companies are allowed to charge. There are thousands of different credit cards offered, so be very selective and "mine your field of diamonds."

There are major differences in the manner in which interest can be compounded on credit cards. Compounded interest can significantly affect the cost of borrowing money. Interest can be compounded daily or monthly and there are different ways that credit cards calculate the balance on which the interest can be applied. Credit card debt is often called revolving debt because interest that is earned on a principal balance is added back to the balance on which interest can then again accrue. Simply put, the issuers earn interest on interest which makes paying off the balance a very timely process and an uphill struggle.

Balance/Interest Calculation Procedures

Following are interest calculation methods that can influence the effective rate of interest that a consumer pays. If the balance is paid on time every month, the method that issuers use to charge interest should not matter. If there is a running balance from billing cycle to billing cycle you should be aware of how your credit card calculates the balance on which interest accrues. Most creditors charge interest based on the Average Daily Balance (including new purchases) method. Following is a summary of how they apply interest:

Average Daily Balance (Including New Purchases)

The credit card issuer adds the balances of every day in the billing cycle. Each daily balance includes new purchases that the consumer makes on that day. The issuer subtracts the amount(s) of any credits and payments that are made for each day. They divide the total of the daily balances by the number of days in the billing cycle to get the average daily balance. The issuer then applies the interest rate to the average daily balance that was calculated.

Other factors influencing interest accrual:

Average Daily Balance (Excluding New Purchases)

The issuer does not include new purchases when calculating the average daily balance.

Two-Cycle Average Daily Balance (Including New Purchases)

The issuer adds the average daily balance for the current billing cycle and the previous billing cycle and charges interest on the combined sum. New purchases are included in each of the daily balances. Credits and payments are deducted from the daily balances.

Two-Cycle Average Daily Balance (Excluding New Purchases)

The issuer adds the average daily balance for the current billing cycle and the previous billing cycle and charges interest on the combined sum. New purchases are not included in each of the daily balances. Credits and payments are deducted from the daily balances.

THE FINE PRINT- WHAT TO LOOK FOR

Misleading Balance Transfer Solicitations- Be very careful of telephone solicitors that offer low interest credit cards. Telemarketers solicit business using a low interest introductory rate offer and lead you to assume that the low interest rate is applicable to the whole balance. After receiving and using the card, you find out that the low interest rate is not applied at all, or is applied to only the balance that is transferred to the new card and normal purchases are subject to a high interest rate. Telephone solicitors may ask for your social security number, to get you approved faster and "lock you into the deal." Avoid giving your social security number over the telephone. If you are interested in their offer, request they send a cardholder agreement and application so you can review the terms in advance.

Bait and Switch Tactics- Bait and switch tactics are methods used by credit card companies to get you to accept their card. Some credit card marketers call consumers and offer "benefits" such as better interest rates or high available credit limits. When the consumer gets the card, they learn that the terms are not the same as the terms they were offered or the terms are subject to only a short time period.

Teaser Rates- Credit card issuers offer introductory "teaser" rates to entice new clients. Consumers are often unaware that the "teaser" rate applies only for a certain time period and then the interest rate increases (usually after 3-6 months.) The consumer is "teased" into acquiring the card by the low, short-lived, interest rate. Details on "teaser rate" offers are usually found in very small print on the credit card application or agreement.

Understanding the following terms will enable you to minimize the costs of credit card use:

Credit Card Grace Period

The grace period is the period during which purchases that are made can be repaid without finance charges being accessed. Typically, credit card issuers offer 25-30 day grace periods but they are often contingent upon the cardholder meeting certain criteria. First, the cardholder has to pay the "balance due" on their last statement on time and in full. Second, the cardholder must pay off the balance due on their next statement on time and in full to avoid the finance charges on purchases made between the two statement dates. In other words, the consumer has to pay off their balances on time and in full for two, consecutive, billing periods or the grace period for new purchases made between the two billing dates does not apply. The interest will start to accrue immediately on new purchases that were made during the time period. Consumers who carry balances on their cards forfeit their grace period.

Minimum Payments-A Debtor's Arch-Enemy

The minimum payment is the minimum amount a cardholder can pay each month to keep the account from falling delinquent. If you carry credit card balances from month to month, you must understand that minimum payment means maximum expense. In most cases, if you make only the minimum payment, the majority of your money will go toward interest (revenue for the credit card company) and a relatively small amount of your money will be applied toward principal (the balance left on the amount that you borrowed). The required minimum payment is calculated by taking a percentage of the existing balance (usually 2%-3%), so the minimum payment decreases as the balance on the account decreases. Minimum payments tempt consumers to procrastinate by not paying immediately for purchases. The ability to make minimum payments gives consumers the false impression that they are in control of their finances. This causes unsuspecting or financially troubled consumers to continue to pay a proportionately large amount of their payment towards interest, which continues the long and costly spiral of getting out of debt. By making minimum payments, consumers increase the cost of interest accrual because they do not make significant decreases in the balances on which interest compounds and continues to "revolve." A debtor's inability to pay more than the minimum payment and break the long spiraling effect is often referred to as "debtors prison." If credit card companies had their wish, everyone would pay minimum payments, which would enable them to make exorbitant amounts of money through extended repayment periods. Paying as much as possible toward credit card balances and reducing interest rates will enable you to get out of debt relatively quickly.

DID YOU KNOW? IF YOUR MINIMUM PAYMENT IS 2% OF THE BALANCE AND THE INTEREST RATE IS 24%, YOU WILL BE MAKING NO PROGRESS ON PAYING DOWN THE BALANCE. THE INTEREST THAT ACCRUES WILL BE EQUAL TO THE MONTHLY PAYMENT.

The following charts (Figures 4.1 and 4.2) demonstrate how increasing a monthly credit card payment from 2% to 3% of the original balance will decrease the payoff time and the total accumulated interest.

Annual Fees

Some credit card companies charge an annual fee, while others do not. Credit cards that charge an annual fee may offer lower interest rates. If you allow balances to carry over from one month to the next, the savings from a low interest rate card with an annual fee may overcome the cost of the yearly fee. If you rarely use your credit card or pay the balance off on a monthly basis, consider a card that does not charge a yearly fee. Annual fees vary but are usually in the range of $15 to $100 per year. They are automatically billed to your

Figure 4.1   PAYMENT SCHEDULE CHART #1

Assuming a $4,500 balance, 17.5% interest, and monthly payments of 2%($90) of the original balance.

Monthly Payment Number	Balance Owed	Monthly Payment	Interest Accumulated
1	$4,500	$90	$65
2	$4.475	$90	$131
3	$4,451	$90	$196
4	$4,426	$90	$260
5	$4,400	$90	$325
6	$4,375	$90	$389
7	$4,349	$90	$452
8	$4,322	$90	$516
9	$4,296	$90	$578
10	$4,268	$90	$641
20	$3,974	$90	$1,243
40	$3,243	$90	$2,300
80	$967	$90	$3,592
91	$75 (last payment)	$90	$3,677

Summary: Repaying debt at 2% ($90) of the original balance per month would take 91 months and would cost $3,677 in interest.

Figure 4.2 PAYMENT SCHEDULE CHART #2

Assuming a $4,500 balance, 17.5% interest, and monthly payments of 3%($135) of the original balance.

Monthly Payment Number	Balance Owed	Monthly Payment	Interest Accumulated
1	$4,500	$135	$65
2	$4.430	$135	$130
3	$4,360	$135	$194
4	$4,289	$135	$257
5	$4,217	$135	$319
6	$4,144	$135	$380
7	$4,070	$135	$440
8	$3,995	$135	$499
9	$3,919	$135	$557
10	$3,842	$135	$613
20	$3,005	$135	$1,114
30	$2,038	$135	$1,484
40	$922	$135	$1,702
47	$40 (last payment)	$135	$1,751

Summary: Repaying debt at 3% ($135) of the original balance per month would take 47 months and would cost $1,751 in interest.

Notice: By paying 3% ($135) instead of 2% ($90) of the original balance ($4,500) monthly, your credit cards would be paid off 44 months (3 years and 8 months) faster and total interest savings would be $1,926.

card at the yearly anniversary.

Penalty Fees- Late and Over-limit

Most credit card issuers reserve the right to charge penalty fees to consumers who do not meet the obligations of their credit card agreement. Penalty fees are very expensive relative to a consumer's balance and can be a major obstacle in reducing balances. Penalty fees are added to the balance, which enables the issuer to earn interest on them. Smart consumers are aware of their due dates and credit limits, and monitor their statements carefully to detect penalty fees. If you are assessed penalty fees, call the credit card issuer and request that the fees be waived. Credit card companies will often waive penalty fees for good paying clients.

Late Fees

Credit card issuers charge a late fee when a consumer fails to make a monthly payment by their due date. Late fees usually range from $10 to $35. Some card issuers charge late fees based on a percentage of the balance owed.

Over-limit Fees

Over-limit fees are charged when a consumer's balance is above their credit limit. Accrued interest and late fees can send a consumer over their credit limit. Over-limit fees usually range from $10 to $30.

Cash Advances

Cash advances allow consumers to borrow cash on their credit cards. Usually there are separate limits and higher interest rates that are applicable to cash advances. The convenience of cash advances make them a grave danger to consumers with questionable spending habits because it makes obtaining additional cash as simple as going to an automatic teller machine (ATM). Credit card issuers often entice consumers by mailing "convenience checks", which when cashed, accrue interest at the same high rate, as a cash advance. Unlike most credit card purchases, interest on a cash advance usually starts to accrue from the date of the transaction. Some credit issuers charge fees on cash advances according to how much money they lend. These fees usually range anywhere from 2-4% of the amount of money that the cardholder borrows. Review your statements. If you are paying interest on a cash advance try to pay off the balance as soon as possible.

DID YOU KNOW? *MOST CREDITORS WILL NOT ALLOW YOU TO EARMARK PAYMENTS IN EXCESS OF THE MINIMUM PAYMENT TO YOUR CASH ADVANCES. ISSUERS HAVE THEIR OWN POLICIES ON HOW OVERPAYMENTS ARE DISTRIBUTED. SOME APPLY THE AMOUNT OVER THE MINIMUM TO NORMAL PURCHASES FIRST (LOWER INTEREST RATE). OTHERS DISTRIBUTE THE OVERAGE PROPORTIONATELY AMONGST THE PURCHASING BALANCE AND CASH ADVANCE BALANCE.*

Understanding Your Monthly Credit Card Statement

The following chart **(Figure 4.3)** is an example of a credit card billing statement. In addition to the information that is included on it, a typical statement would include an itemized summary of the transactions that occurred within the billing period. An address would be printed on the reverse side of statement at which to write if you want to contest information as reported on the statement (See The Fair Credit Billing Act below).

THE FAIR CREDIT BILLING ACT (FCBA)

In 1975, the Fair Credit Billing Act was passed through Congress. The purpose of the legislation was to create guidelines for resolution of disputes that resulted from consumers disagreeing with information that was reflected on their credit card statement. On the reverse side of a credit card statement, an address is provided to which the consumer can write and dispute information on their statement that they feel is incorrect. The cardholder must submit a letter within 60 days of receiving the billing statement that they believe to be incorrect. The following information must be included in the letter:

- The name of the cardholder
- The cardholder's address
- The cardholder's account number
- A summary of the reason for the dispute with information specific to the date and the amount of the transaction being disputed

Fig. 4.3 HOW TO READ A CREDIT CARD STATEMENT

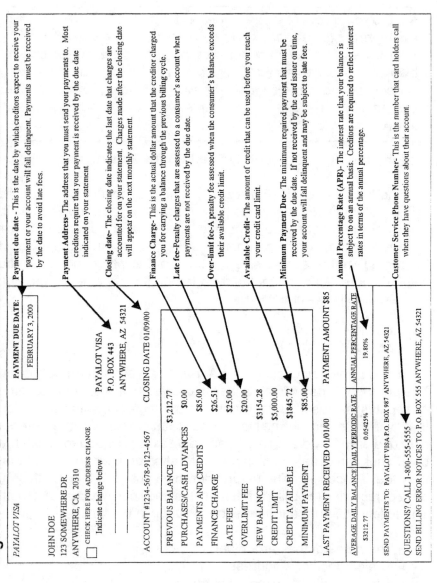

Payment due date - This is the date by which creditors expect to receive your payment or your account will fall delinquent. Payments must be received by the date to avoid late fees.

Payment Address- The address that you must send your payments to. Most creditors require that your payment is received by the due date indicated on your statement

Closing date- The closing date indicates the last date that charges are accounted for on your statement. Charges made after the closing date will appear on the next monthly statement.

Finance Charge- This is the actual dollar amount that the creditor charged you for carrying a balance through the previous billing cycle.

Late fee-Penalty charges that are assessed to a consumer's account when payments are not received by the due date.

Over-limit fee-A penalty fee assessed when the consumer's balance exceeds their available credit limit.

Available Credit- The amount of credit that can be used before you reach your credit card limit.

Minimum Payment Due- The minimum required payment that must be received by the due date. If not received by the card issuer on time, your account will fall delinquent and may be subject to late fees.

Annual Percentage Rate (APR)- The interest rate that your balance is subject to on an annual basis. Creditors are required to reflect interest rates in terms of the annual percentage.

Customer Service Phone Number- This is the number that card holders call when they have questions about their account.

PAYALOT VISA

PAYMENT DUE DATE:
FEBRUARY 3, 2000

JOHN DOE
123 SOMEWHERE DR.
ANYWHERE, CA 20310

☐ CHECK HERE FOR ADDRESS CHANGE
Indicate change below

PAYALOT VISA
P.O. BOX 443
ANYWHERE, AZ 54321

ACCOUNT #1234-5678-9123-4567   CLOSING DATE 01/09/00

PREVIOUS BALANCE	$3,212.77
PURCHASES/CASH ADVANCES	$0.00
PAYMENTS AND CREDITS	$85.00
FINANCE CHARGE	$26.51
LATE FEE	$25.00
OVERLIMIT FEE	$20.00
NEW BALANCE	$3154.28
CREDIT LIMIT	$5,000.00
CREDIT AVAILABLE	$1845.72
MINIMUM PAYMENT	$85.00

LAST PAYMENT RECEIVED 01/01/00   PAYMENT AMOUNT $85

AVERAGE DAILY BALANCE	DAILY PERIODIC RATE	ANNUAL PERCENTAGE RATE
$3212.77	0.05425%	19.80%

SEND PAYMENTS TO: PAYALOT VISA P.O. BOX 987 ANYWHERE, AZ 54321

QUESTIONS? CALL 1-800-555-5555
SEND BILLING ERROR NOTICES TO: P.O. BOX 555 ANYWHERE, AZ 54321

The credit issuer has 30 days in which to acknowledge receipt of the dispute letter. The consumer does not have to pay the portion of the bill that is in dispute while it is being investigated. During the investigation, the credit issuer may not report derogatory information to credit agencies concerning information that is relative to the disputed item. After investigating the dispute, if the credit card issuer determines that the information, as originally reflected on the statement is correct, they must send a letter to the cardholder explaining that they found no error in the information as it was recorded on the statement. If requested by the cardholder, the creditor must provide copies of information that they used to support that the information, as originally reported, was correct. The credit issuer must advise the cardholder of the amount due on their account and the due date by which they need to remit payment. If the cardholder does not pay by the due date, information may be reported to the credit bureau.

If the credit card issuer determines that information, as found on the original statement, was reported in error, they must correct the error by crediting the account. In addition, they must provide a letter that confirms their error and summarizes the corrections that will be made to repair it.

Holding your own in the Credit Card Game

Playing Hard Ball: Negotiating Your Own Terms

When dealing with credit card issuers, understand that the name of the game for the issuer is making money on interest. You can control the game because they cannot make money if you do not use their card. If you have good credit and a good payment history, the game is played on your field because the creditors who don't have your business will want it, and the creditors that do have your business will not want to lose it. It is often effective to play your card against the competition. If you want a lower interest rate, request that the card issuer reduce the interest and advise them that if they do not reduce it, you will transfer the balance to a card on which you were offered a lower introductory interest rate. It often helps to remind the issuer that you are a good paying customer. Come in with a game plan and be specific on the interest rate that you desire.

Obtaining a better interest rate may be a "see-saw" battle. If you start low with the interest rate that you request, it will give you room to negotiate and compromise at a favorable rate if the creditor rejects your offer. You cannot be penalized for requesting a lower rate so be firm but reasonable. It is wise to ask for a rate that is similar to an introductory rate. Try to "lock in" to a rate that will not change after a given time period. If your request for a better interest rate is denied, request to speak to a supervisor. Often representatives are not given the authority to reduce interest rates so their response is a simple "no" but if you get to a supervisor, they may have the authority to reduce interest rates.

Shopping Interest Rates

Acquire low interest credit cards and transfer balances

Shopping around is another angle to take toward credit card repayment. Used in combination with effective budgeting and aggressive repayment planning, shopping around enables you to use a three pronged approach. You should always be aware of the interest rate you are paying on your credit cards. It is wise to transfer high interest

Go Fishing For Good Rates

rate credit card balances to lower interest rate cards if your credit limit will allow you to do so. When shopping around, it is important to account for the way that the balance is being calculated on which interest can accrue (see Balance/Interest calculation procedures on page 44). Depending on which calculation method the credit card uses, it may drive up the effective rate of interest that you are required to pay. It is important to keep track of the expiration date on introductory interest rate offers. If you are unsure of when the term of the introductory interest rate expires, read the credit card agreement (it is probably in the small print) or call the issuer. Be very careful of misleading balance transfer solicitations. Be sure that you have been approved for an introductory rate offer on another card at the credit limit and terms that your desire, prior to closing your old account. Pre-approved offers are not 100% guaranteed. Once approved, and your balance has been transferred, close your old account so you are not tempted to charge up more debt and overextend your finances.

CHAPTER 5

EFFECTIVELY HANDLING CREDITORS AND DEBT COLLECTORS

CHAPTER 5

EFFECTIVELY HANDLING CREDITORS AND DEBT COLLECTORS

Depending on your situation and the amount of money available for distribution to your creditors, consider working out a payment solution on your own. There are two different types of collectors that may call you. If your account is not severely behind (less than four to six months behind), you will probably be getting calls and collection letters from the original credit institution that offered the line of credit. The other type of collector that you may deal with is a third party collector who represents a recovery or collection agency. Generally speaking, dealing with the original creditor is a more pleasant experience than dealing with third party collectors. With knowledge and understanding on how to handle collectors, dealing with both types of creditors can be handled effectively.

Normally, the further delinquent the account, the more collection pressure you will experience. When an account reaches a certain delinquency threshold it will be transferred or sold from the original creditor to a collection or recovery agency. At approximately 4-6 months delinquency, the original creditor will usually charge an account off and sell it at a discount to a collection agency or recovery agency. When charged off, the original creditor considers the balance to be "uncollectible" by their standards and they remove the uncollectible balances from other active collectible account records. Generally speaking, when an account is charged off, it means that the original creditor will no longer attempt to collect money that is owed and they will usually hire a collections or recovery agency or sell the account at a discount. In most cases, when an account is charged off, the interest stops accruing on the balance and penalty fees are no longer applied. However, legal fees and processing fees can be added which may inflate the balance that the debtor owes. The original creditor usually has a vested interest in preventing the account from being charged off because charge-offs are considered to be a loss. However, if the account does charge off, it can be written off as a loss and the creditor can offset the loss by using it as a corporate write-off. Original creditors are usually more pleasant and proactive in devising repayment arrangements with the debtor.

When an account is turned over to a collection agency, the consumer often faces more intense collection attempts that may border on harassment. The aggressive tactics are designed to cause the consumer to overestimate the power of the collector and the risk of legal ramifications. From the collector's perspective, they have to be more aggressive because, the fact that the account charged-off indicates that normal collection attempts were not effective. They resort to scare tactics to create a sense of urgency but many of their implied threats are unfounded. Third party collectors are often paid bonuses or commissions based on the total amount of debt that they collect and their performance is usually evaluated based on their ability to meet strict quotas. The incentives and the pressure that they are under tend to "add more fuel to their collecting fire." When dealing with collectors, try to remain calm and avoid reacting to their threats and implications. If the collector senses that you are afraid or concerned, they will often use your emotions against you. This may lead to a scenario in which you pledge to pay more than you can afford, and short change your other financial obligations.

It is important to realize that unsecured creditors can adopt more drastic methods of collection such as wage and bank account assignment, and attachment of personal property. Their decision to take more drastic collection measures is determined by the cost that they will incur and the time frame that it would take to experience a benefit. For relatively small debts, it is usually not worth the time and effort that it takes to pursue drastic measures because the creditor's gain from doing so will probably not overcome the costs. When determining how to react to collection threats, the debtor should compare the possibility of the creditor taking extra measures to collect the debt, to the risk associated with not taking the threats seriously.

In most cases, creditors will not resort to suing a debtor as a method of collecting on a debt until they have exhausted routine collection efforts.

GUIDELINES TO FOLLOW WHEN DEALING WITH COLLECTORS

⇨ Try to avoid paying by personal check. If you send a personal check, the creditor will know where you bank and will acquire your account number. There is often personal information on checks such as your address, telephone number, and the name of other friends or family members who may be making a payment for you. Collectors may use the information on your check to obtain additional information or attach your bank account.

⇨ Collectors may try to bully you into giving personal information over the phone. You do not have to give personal information over the phone. If a collector asks for employment, bank account, or personal information, don't give it to them. They may use the information to attach your wages or bank account.

⇨ If you are sending payment to a collector and do not want them to know your address, do not include a return address. Though not giving your address can be an effective way of avoiding creditors, it may work against you because you will not receive notice about the status on your account.

LEGAL STEPS COLLECTORS MUST TAKE BEFORE ATTACHING (GARNISHING) WAGES OR BANK ACCOUNTS

Collectors often threaten or make references to garnishing your wages. This is often an effective scare tactic because most consumers are unaware of the measures that must be taken to garnish wages or fear the embarrassment of having a boss or coworker know they are delinquent on debts. It is illegal for a collector to tell you they are going to sue you as a means of getting you to pay the debt, if they do not plan on doing so. A collection agency cannot garnish your wages without going through the required legal process. For a third party collector to garnish your wages they first have to sue you. Thus, you should not necessarily believe a collector if they

61

tell you your wages are going to be garnished unless you have a prior judgment entered against you by a court. A judgment is a legal determination made by the court affirming that a particular party owes another party a specified amount of money.

Much like garnishment, judgments do not appear out of thin air. To have a judgment entered against you, a formal written complaint or petition must, first, be issued by a court and served via certified mail or by an official server. To serve the papers, the creditor may hire a process server or have a local sheriff serve the papers. If you receive a complaint, you will be required to answer the complaint within the specified time period by completing a response explaining why you want to contest the lawsuit. If you do not complete a response to the complaint or if you do respond to the complaint but do not appear for the court date, there is a risk of having a default judgment placed against you. If you call the creditor, you may be able to negotiate a repayment plan and the creditor may agree to suspend the lawsuit. After responding to the complaint, a court date will be arranged and you will be required to appear and give information to support your situation. It is often helpful for a consumer to demonstrate, to the court, that there was a particular hardship that caused their inability to pay on the debt. It may also be helpful to show that you have, proactively, made efforts to make payment arrangements, such as enrolling with a credit-counseling agency **(see chapter 9)** or establishing a repayment arrangement with the creditor. Once a judgment is awarded against a consumer, the creditor who filed the initial complaint may adopt more aggressive measures to reclaim the money that has been determined as rightfully theirs. These measures include wage or bank account garnishment, or attachment of personal property. Laws vary, state to state, with regard to the extent to which a judgement creditor may pursue personal assets. Understanding the laws that govern debt collectors will help you to keep things in perspective and control the flow of a conversation with a collector.

Settling Debts

In some circumstances, you may be able to "settle" your debts for less than what is owed. In some cases, debtors can negotiate settlements for 50%-70% on the dollar. The likelihood of negotiating a settlement is dependent on the type of debt, the repayment record on the debt, and individual circumstances surrounding a consumer.

Settling debt is usually only possible if the debt is unsecured debt (debt that does not involve collateral.) Some examples of unsecured debts that may be settled upon are credit cards, medical bills, personal loans, and balances that debtors are legally liable for after foreclosure or repossession. Creditors have no reason to engage in settlement negotiations on secured debt because they can repossess the property that is backing the loan and resell it to recoup the money that was loaned. In rare cases, secured automobile loans may be settled upon if the car backing the loan has lost most of its value and is not worth repossessing. Generally speaking, creditors will not settle on debt on which you are current. However, on unsecured debt, creditors are willing to settle as a way of minimizing the loss that they expect to have to incur on debt that is difficult to collect upon. If an account is current, the creditor has no reason to believe that they have to take a loss, because it appears the debtor can still afford to pay their bills. On rare occasions, creditors may be willing to settle debt that is current. One example would be a situation in which a debtor becomes sick or injured and unable to work to pay on their debt. In circumstances like these, the creditor would probably require that the debtor substantiate the reason for the settlement by asking for documentation to support the unusual circumstances.

Tips for settling your debts

Settling debt is a like playing poker. If the creditors are entertaining the thought of agreeing to a settlement on your debt, it is a good indicator that you "hold the upper hand." Once you know they will settle, make sure you get the lowest possible settlement terms. Following are guidelines to follow when attempting to settle a debt.

Go into negotiations with a game plan.

Remember that you are in control. The game is played on your field. They want the money and you are the one that can give it to them. By the time you get around to settling the debt, your balance may be inflated with legal fees, interest, and penalty fees. Try to use the amount of debt that you borrowed as a worst case scenario for settlement. In other words, try not to settle for more than the principal amount that you borrowed. Attempt to settle for as small a percentage of the money that you borrowed as possible.

63

Bid low to start.

When you first engage in negotiations with creditors, start low on your settlement figure. If you overbid on the settlement offer, you may cost yourself a lot of money. Settling is often a "see-saw battle of wills" that takes some time. You may have to come back to the bargaining table with several settlement offers before finally coming to an agreement with the creditor.

Don't let the creditor control the situation.

The creditor may try to play hard ball and offer you a settlement agreement that does not save a lot of money. Do not be quick to settle on their first offer and remember, they are probably trying to show you their best "poker face." However, the debt is yours and you are the one who holds the cards. Calling their bluff is often very effective. If you call their bluff and tell them that their offer is not good enough, chances are, they will still come back with a better offer. Sometimes it is helpful to "walk away" from the bargaining table, which may cause the creditor to become more desperate.

Let the creditor know that they are one of many and bankruptcy is one of your options.

Let your creditors know that they are just one of many and you are making a last ditch effort to repay them. Tell them that you are committed to prioritizing paying settlements to the creditors who cooperate with you. Tell them if things do not work out, you may have to file bankruptcy. Mentioning bankruptcy cannot hurt because the creditor will realize if you do file bankruptcy, they will get nothing, which may make them more content to get whatever they can.

Substantiate your reason for needing to settle.

If you can demonstrate that your finances are unstable, your creditors will be more likely to settle at a lower amount. Sometimes the verbal threat of bankruptcy does not work by itself and you need to support that your finances are on "shaky ground." If you don't substantiate your position, the creditor may assume that you are bluffing to get the best possible settlement. Maybe you are bluffing,

64

but if you are not, proving it to the creditor may cause them to give you better settlement terms. If times are tough, it is often helpful to send a letter or budget form demonstrating that your income is not sufficient to satisfy all of your obligations. If your obligations are falling behind due to circumstances that are out of your control such as medical conditions, it is often helpful to send documents that support the circumstances that you have been forced into dealing with. If you have lost your job, they might not be sympathetic because they may not feel it is a situation out of your control. From their perspective it is still your responsibility to get a new job.

Keep good records and follow up.

Always keep a record of your conversations with the collection representatives. Often, when dealing with a recovery department on a settlement, you will be dealing with more than one person. If you are not getting straight answers, be firm and request to speak to the person that makes the decisions. When dealing with creditors, always confirm a date by which you can expect a decision and follow up if you don't get a response by the agreed upon date. If you confirm a decision date in advance, it will not seem as though you are desperate if you call to follow up after the date has passed. In other words, the burden of meeting the deadline is in their hands which gives you good reason to follow up with them.

Try to make the settlement as "credit report friendly" as possible.

As part of the settlement agreement, request that the creditor remove all references to the account from your credit report. If they won't, ask them to simply report the account as "paid" instead of "settled" and remove all references to delinquency, charge-off, collections, or repossession. Your success will depend on the policy of the creditor that you are dealing with. In worst case, the account may appear on your credit report as "settled" or "bad debt" and reflect references to the former status of the account such as delinquencies, charge-off, collections, or repossession. At least you will have gained by paying your debt off at a discount. It will show that you took responsibility and were committed to paying your debt off regardless of the fact that the debt was settled.

65

Get all agreements in writing.

Do not ever trust a creditor's word. Always get any form of settlement agreement in writing from the creditor. When you get the agreement in writing you should be sure to include a date by which payment must be received from you for the settlement amount to be valid. Include all specifications concerning how the settled upon account will be reported to the credit bureaus. Send the settlement funds and a copy of the agreement back to the creditor via certified mail, return receipt, so you have confirmation that your payment was received on time.

THE FAIR DEBT COLLECTIONS PRACTICES ACT

Knowing the rules will help you play the collection game.

You are protected by The Fair Debt Collection Practices Act, which is federal law that protects consumers from harassment and abusive collection styles. The Fair Debt Collection Practices Act applies to collection efforts that are employed by persons other than the original creditor "that regularly collect debts owed to others." The FDCPA applies to third party collectors who have purchased accounts or been hired by an "original creditor" to collect on a debt. Original credit institutions are not required to abide by the provisions set forth by the act. Understanding the Fair Debt Collection Practices Act and letting the creditors know that you understand your rights is one of the most effective ways of dealing with collectors and their unsubstantiated threats.

FDCPA When a debt collector calls:

When a collector contacts you, at some point in the conversation they must advise you that they are calling from a collection agency. They are required to identify the name of the original creditor and the amount of the balance on the account that is being collected upon. This is important because it allows you to determine whether it is a bill on which you feel your are responsible for paying or on which you have a dispute. If the collector was not required to advise you of the balance and original creditor, you might pay on a bill that

You're Late!

you are not legally responsible for or you might pay more than you are legally required to. The collector must advise you that the purpose of the call is to collect a debt and that the information provided by you will be used for the purpose of collecting a debt. The collector is also required to advise that you reserve the right to dispute the debt within 30 days.

FDCPA Restrictions governing debt collectors:

Tactics that are not permitted:

- The debt collector cannot repeatedly call you.
- If you request that collectors do not call you at work, they must stop.
- Collectors cannot use foul language or threaten a consumer with violence, seizure of assets, or imprisonment. They cannot use language that is insulting, discriminatory or belittling.
- Without obtaining your permission, collectors are not permitted to tell any person other than yourself, a cosigner, your spouse, or your attorney that you owe a debt.

- The debt collector cannot publish your name and the nature of the debt. They may not threaten to harm your reputation as a measure to collect a debt.
- A debt collector cannot call you or in any way contact you before 8:00 a.m. or after 9 p.m. in accordance with your local time zone.
- A collection agency cannot deposit a postdated check prior to the date on the check.
- A collection agency cannot collect any amount greater than your debt, unless allowed by law.

Rules governing false representation:

- Debt collectors cannot misrepresent who they are. Collectors may not pretend to be someone else or to represent a business or agency that they are not affiliated with. Collectors cannot falsely imply they are attorneys or government representatives. They cannot indicate that forms or letters sent to you are legal forms if they are not.
- Collectors cannot falsely imply that you have committed a crime. They cannot threaten that you will be arrested if you do not pay a debt.
- Debt collectors may not offer false information to get you to pay a debt. In other words, collectors may not inform you or write to you advising that they are going to sue you, garnish your wages, or attach personal property if they do not actually have the intent to do so.
- Collectors cannot falsely represent that they work for a credit bureau.

What to do if collection activity becomes unbearable:

In accordance with the FDCPA, if dealing with third party collectors becomes unbearable you may send Cease and Desist Notification to them, which requires them to stop contacting you. Frustrated consumers do this when there is no end in sight to the constant calls and emotional distress that unrelenting collection attempts may be causing. When a debt collection agency receives Cease and Desist Notification, they cannot communicate further with the consumer with respect to the debt:

"except—
1) to advise the consumer that the debt collector's efforts are being terminated
2) to notify the consumer that the debt collector or creditor may invoke specific remedies which are ordinarily invoked by such debt collector or creditor: or
3) where applicable, to notify the consumer that the debt collector or creditor intends to invoke a specific remedy."

Cease and Desist notification is applicable to third party collectors only. If you send a Cease and Desist letter to an original creditor, they are not required to refrain from calling you and they may respond negatively and heighten their collection efforts. It is important to remember that sending Cease and Desist Notification does not pardon you from repayment of a debt. The fact that your life will be relatively more peaceful does not mean that your obligations have gone away. If you send Cease and Desist notification to your creditors, you should continue to make consistent monthly payments to establish that you are committed to paying back the balance owed. If possible, try to pay about 2% of the balance on a monthly basis. If you do not establish that you are committed to repaying the debt, and the creditors cannot contact you, they may be prompted to try to collect on the debt by suing you.

AS A SAFEGUARD, IT IS BEST TO HAVE CEASE AND DESIST NOTIFICATION DELIVERED BY CERTIFIED MAIL, RETURN RECEIPT REQUESTED, BECAUSE YOU WILL HAVE CONCRETE PROOF THAT THE COLLECTOR RECEIVED IT.

Below is an example of a Cease and Desist Letter:

December 5, 1999

Collect My Debt Collection Agency
2300 Daffodil Lane
West Debtville, AK 24252

RE: Account # 6754-7685

Dear Collect My Debt Collections:

Under provision of the **Fair Debt Collection Practices Act, 15 U.S.C. 1592 et. seq.,** you are hereby notified to **Cease and Desist** in any and all attempts to collect the above referenced debt through direct contact with me. Your failure to do so will result in charges being filed against you with the state and federal regulatory agencies empowered with enforcement. My intent is to fulfill my obligations to your organization as soon as it is feasible.

Very truly yours,

John Doe (include your signature)

CHAPTER 6

CREDIT BUREAU REPORTING

CHAPTER 6

CREDIT BUREAU REPORTING

AN OVERVIEW OF CREDIT REPORTING

In their efforts to evaluate consumer credit worthiness, creditors depend on credit reporting bureaus to supply reports that provide more specific consumer information. Most creditors have automated systems that allow them direct access to credit reports from the different credit bureaus. Credit bureaus contain personal information, account history information, legal information, and information about inquiries. Some lending institutions use more than one type of credit report because they are required to as a measure of meeting lending requirements. Others use multiple sources to ensure that they are getting a more comprehensive background on a consumer's credit history. When a consumer completes a credit application, many creditors submit the personal information that is on the credit application to credit bureaus. This is how the credit bureaus compile personal information such as a consumer's name, employment information, address, social security number, marital status, and telephone number. By using a credit report, the creditors will be able to cross-reference the information that the consumer provides on their application with the information that the credit bureau accumulated through other credit applications. Many credit institutions hire companies that research and verify that the information on a consumer's credit application is accurate.

If you have an account with a creditor that reports to a credit

73

bureau, your credit report will reflect a payment and account history. The information that a credit bureau reports regarding a consumer's history on a credit account is referred to as a "tradeline." On your credit report, there should be a "tradeline" for every creditor that reports account information to the credit bureau that is providing the report. Following is a summary of the information that is normally included in a "tradeline" on a consumer's credit report:

> *Name of the creditor*
> *Account number (usually incomplete or coded for security purposes)*
> *Type of account (installment loan or revolving)*
> *Balance owed*
> *Summarized payment history*
> *Date the account was opened*
> *Credit limit*
> *Cosigners on the account*
> *Date information was last reported to the bureau*

In addition to the information that is normally reported, a "tradeline" may indicate the following:

> If the account has been included in a bankruptcy proceeding
> If there has been a repossession of collateral
> If an account has been charged off
> If an account has been turned over to collections

Not all credit institutions report to credit bureaus, but most of them do. Most credit bureaus report payment history in 30-day payment intervals because 30-day periods are reflective of monthly billing cycles and payment installments. Policies vary amongst creditors with regard to the threshold at which they report delinquency to the credit bureau. Some creditors do not report delinquency until the consumer's account reaches 60 days past due, while others report delinquency at 30 days past due. Some creditors do not report any account history to the credit bureau unless there is delinquency on the account. The "historical method" of reporting delinquency on your credit report will reflect the number of times that you fell more than 30, 60, 90, and 120 days behind on your payment obligations. Other credit reports utilize a rating system that assigns a "status" for each 30-day range of delinquency. This method is referred to as the "simple method of payment." An R-1 rating indicates an account that was current or paid "as agreed." An R-2 indicates that a consumer paid 30 days or more after the due date but less than 60 days after the due date. An R-3 indicates that the bill was paid 60 or more days after the due date but less than 90 days past due. An R-4 indicates that the consumer paid 90 or more days past due but less than 120 days. R-5 indicates that a consumer paid 120 or more days past their due date. R-7 usually means that a creditor repossessed collateral on the account and R-8 reflects that the account was turned over to collections. R-9 can be used to reflect many different statuses on an account. It may be used to reflect that a debt was discharged in bankruptcy, repossessed, foreclosed upon, or in collections.

Credit reports often include a section that provides information that is considered public record such as tax liens, judgements, and arrests and convictions. Credit reports also give records of inquiries. Inquiries are records that reflect requests made by creditors to a credit bureau for a consumers credit report. Inquiries indicate the name of the creditor that requested the report and the date on which the report was requested.

Following are factors that are of particular interest to lenders:

⇨Do the applicants have a stable job? How many years have they been at their place of employment? Do they have a responsible job title?

⇨Do the applicants have a stable style of living? Have they been at their place of residence for five years or more? Do they own or rent their home?

⇨Do the applicants exhibit stability with their finances? Do they have a checking and savings account? Do they have many recent inquiries?

⇨Do the applicants have a good payment history on existing and previous lines of credit? Do they have a past credit history free of judgements, bankruptcies, charged off accounts, or other signs of financial mismanagement?

⇨Do the applicants have a favorable debt to income ratio? (Debt to income ratio is a comparison of your outstanding indebtedness to the income that you have to support debt repayment). Does it appear as though they are overextended on credit?

CREDIT SCORING

Creditors often rely on credit scores to help them determine the risk of lending to consumers. The information on a consumers credit file may be used to compile a score that will be used to determine if a consumer is granted a loan or line of credit. If a decision is made to grant a line of credit to a consumer, the credit score may be used to determine the interest rate that will be applied to the loan or line of credit. Generally speaking, the riskier it is to lend to a consumer, the lower the chances are that the consumer will be approved for the line of credit and the higher the interest rate at which the consumer will be required to repay the debt if they are approved. Many lenders have "in house" scoring systems but they also rely on scoring models that are provided by credit reporting bureaus. Different credit bureaus use different credit scoring models, but the standards of determining a consumer's credit worthiness are consistent from model to model and they are based on the Fair Isaac Company's scoring criteria. The scoring system that is used may be termed a "Beacon," "Empirica," or a "FICO" score depending on what credit bureau is supplying the score **(see Chapter 7 - ordering and reviewing your credit report)**. Some lenders rely upon "merged" credit reports that provide a compilation of consumer account and credit scoring information from more than one reporting bureau.

THE FAIR CREDIT REPORTING ACT

Unfortunately, credit problems are not only limited to our immediate ability to manage our finances and make payments on time. If you were past due on credit obligations and brought your account(s) back to a current status, the damage that was done while you were behind may follow you for a while. Being current on credit obligations bodes well for you in that it demonstrates your ability to afford to meet immediate obligations, but the creditors are also interested in your "past track record" because they fear that there may be a correlation between past history and future expectancy. To remove derogatory information from your credit, your credit often has to stand the test of time. You can improve your credit by bringing your accounts current and remaining current on your obligations. Staying current on your obligations demonstrates that your finances are more stable and that you can effectively manage your finances and your debt. To understand the rules that govern how long information can stay on your credit report, you need to understand the Fair Credit Reporting Act.

The Fair Credit Reporting Act created rules that govern reporting of information as it appears on credit reports. Initially, the parameters of reporting guidelines in the Fair Debt Collection Practices Act were vague. Most information could remain on a consumer's credit report for approximately seven years (bankruptcy could be reported for up to ten years) but the limits of when the seven-year period began and ended were not clearly defined. In 1996 the Consumer Credit Reporting Reform Act was created to clarify the credit reporting guidelines that are set forth in the Fair Credit Reporting Act.

In accordance with the Fair Credit Reporting Act, the following information that was reported to a credit bureau on or after January 1, 1998 is not permitted to appear on a consumer's credit report. Information that was reported to a credit bureau earlier than January 1, 1998 may not be subject to the same requirements.

Bankruptcies that date back more than ten years from the date of entry of the order of relief from or the date of adjudication.

Civil suits, civil judgements, or records of arrest that date back more than seven years from the date of entry or that exceed the statute of limitations.

Paid liens that date back more than seven years from the date of the report.

Accounts that were placed for collection or charged off which date back more than seven years beginning 180 days after the last payment was due prior to the account being turned over to collections or charged off.

Any other derogatory information other than records of conviction for crimes that date back more than seven years from the date of the report.

The preceding guidelines are not applicable for any consumer report to be used in connection with any of the following:

A credit transaction involving or expected to involve a principal amount of $150,000 or more.

Underwriting life insurance, which may be expected to include a value of $150,000 or more.

Pre-screening for employment of any individual at a salary of $75,000 or more.

Other consumer reporting guidelines:

Bankruptcy

For the protection of the consumer, consumer reports are required to meet other guidelines. If the source that provides information regarding a bankruptcy indicates what chapter was filed, the reporting agency must include the chapter on the credit report. Additionally, if a bankruptcy is withdrawn before "final judgment" and the agency has received information confirming that it was withdrawn, the agency must indicate it on the consumer report.

Accounts that are voluntarily closed by the consumer

When including information that is relative to a consumers account on a report, if an agency receives verification that the consumer voluntarily closed the account, they are responsible for indicating on the report, that the consumer voluntarily closed the account.

Disputes

An agency is responsible for noting that there is a dispute over information that is reported on a consumer report if the consumer directly notifies the agency. It is the agency's responsibility to investigate and record the status of the disputed information or delete the information from the consumer report. There is a 30-day time frame that begins on the day the agency receives the formal notice of dispute from the consumer during which the investigation must be completed. The agency is responsible for reviewing all the "relevant information" that a consumer provides but they can end the investigation if the consumer does not provide enough information to support their investigation. The agency may also terminate the investigation if they "reasonably determine" that the dispute is "frivolous" or "irrelevant" and they must notify the consumer within five days. The notification must include the reason for terminating the investigation, and it must identify information that is required to investigate the dispute. When an agency provides notification of the results of an investigation to a consumer, they must include a notice that the consumer has the right to request that the agency submit notification to other agencies through an automated system that enables them to share information with other bureaus. Within five days of receiving notice from the consumer, the agency is responsible for providing notification of the dispute to the source that provided the information that is being disputed. If, during the course of the investigation, the agency receives additional "relevant" information pertaining to the dispute, they are responsible for extending the investigation period for an additional 15 days. The agency does not have to provide a 15 day extension if, during the initial 30 day period, it determines that the information that a consumer has supplied to support their dispute is "inaccurate," "incomplete," or "unverifiable."

If, after investigating the dispute, the agency determines that the furnisher of the disputed information (creditor) provided "inaccurate or incomplete" information, the agency must correct the information as it is reported on the file or delete the incorrect information. An agency must mail written notice to the consumer of the results of the investigation within five business days. The written notice has to include a statement that the investigation is complete and a copy of the consumer report that reflects any changes that resulted from the dispute investigation. It must also include a notice advising that the consumer has the right to add a statement to their file that disputes the "accuracy and completeness of the information" (see following page— "Your right to include a consumer statement"). The agency must provide a confirmation of the consumer's right to have the agency provide notification to any person who previously had received a copy of the incorrect report within 5 business days. Specifically, the agency must submit a copy of the corrected report to any person who received the report within two years prior for employment purposes, and to any person who received the incorrect report "for any other purpose" within six months prior to the correction. If the consumer requests, the bureau is responsible for including a description of the procedure that was used to determine the accuracy and completeness of the information within fifteen days after receiving the request. If an agency deletes information as the result of the dispute within three business days or less from the day that the agency received a notice of dispute from a client, they may notify the consumer by telephone of the deletion. However, within five business days, the agency must provide written confirmation of the deletion and provide a statement that advises the client of the right to have the agency notify (upon request) any parties that previously received an incorrect report.

Reinserting previously deleted material

Information that has previously been deleted from a report file may only be re-added if the creditor who is reporting the information "certifies" that the information to be re-added is "complete and accurate." Within 5 days of the reinsertion of information, the agency must notify the consumer in writing. The agency is responsible for providing information identifying the party that provided the information that lead to the reinsertion of information on a report. The agency must also provide the address and contact information for the party who provided the information, and they must provide notification to the consumer that the consumer has the right "to add a statement disputing the accuracy and completeness of the disputed information." Consumer reporting agencies are responsible for taking "reasonable procedures to prevent the reappearance of information" that has previously been deleted. Agencies that maintain files on a nationwide basis must have an automated system that allows parties who provided the information to the agency (creditors) to be able to report "incomplete or inaccurate information," as determined by the investigation to other reporting agencies.

Your right to include a consumer statement

If you disputed information that appears on your credit report and the credit bureau determines that you have not provided enough information to warrant changing the report or deleting the information, you are entitled to prepare a statement to be added to your credit report. The statement must be limited to 100 words. Preparing a statement will give you an opportunity to fully explain the reason why you are disputing the information despite the fact that you were unable to provide enough supporting evidence to have the information changed or removed.

Guidelines governing how creditors report information to the credit bureau(s):

⇨They cannot report information that they know is incorrect.

⇨They cannot ignore information that contradicts information that they have on file.

⇨They must notify the credit bureau if a debtor disputes information with them.

⇨They must indicate when a consumer voluntarily closes an account.

⇨They must investigate a consumer dispute within 30 days of receiving notice.

CHAPTER 7

UNDERSTANDING CREDIT AND IMPROVING CREDIT WORTHINESS

CHAPTER 7

UNDERSTANDING CREDIT AND IMPROVING CREDIT WORTHINESS

WEIGHING THE EFFECTS OF CREDIT INFORMATION

The impact that credit rating factors can have on evaluation of credit worthiness is relative to the time frame during which they are reported and the relative "maturity" of the consumer's credit history. If derogatory information has been reported to a credit bureau in the recent past, it will most likely weigh heavier against a consumer's credit worthiness than information that was reported a relatively longer time ago. Generally speaking, creditors are more concerned about information in the near past because it is more indicative of the consumer's present financial circumstances. That is not to say, however, that older derogatory information may not effect the outcome of a loan application or the interest or payment terms that are offered on a loan or credit card.

If derogatory information is reported on a consumer who has a "mature," long standing, and otherwise positive credit history, the information will not affect the consumer's credit worthiness or score as much as it would an individual who has a relatively "immature," short, and less comprehensive history. A "mature" history is not only determined by length or account history, it is also determined by the kind of credit that the consumer uses. In other words, positive or negative information concerning a major credit card account (Visa, MasterCard, Discover, or American Express) or installment loan may weigh heavier than information that is reported on a merchant, department store or gas card. Finance company accounts may weigh heavier against a credit score, especially if they were established in the recent past. Finance company loans are regarded as riskier loans that consumers turn to when they run out of conventional options. They are relatively easy to acquire and often require payment of very high interest that drives monthly payments higher. The higher payments can contribute to financial mismanagement and overextension on credit obligations.

IMPROVING YOUR CREDIT SCORE

Ordering and reviewing your credit report

You will never know what is on your credit report unless you check it or get denied for a credit line. Order a copy of your credit report and review it to make sure that all of your personal information and account history information is complete and correct. In accordance with the Fair Credit Reporting Act, if you are turned down for credit, you may obtain a free credit report, provided you request it within 60 days. If you have not been turned down and desire a credit report, it will cost approximately $8. Credit reporting agencies are required to provide trained employees to help consumers interpret information that is found on their report. You can obtain a copy of your credit report by contacting the following credit reporting bureaus:

Experian: (800) 682-7654   credit scoring model: FICO

Equifax: (800) 685-1111   credit scoring model: Beacon

Trans Union:(800) 851-2674   credit scoring model:Empirica

Please Note: It can take up to six weeks to receive a credit report from the major credit bureaus referenced above.

If you would like to use a service that combines information from all three credit bureaus into one easy-to-read format, you can visit:

www.CreditReport411.com or call (800) 227-1479

This service comes with unlimited free access to their credit advisory hotline. This service takes about 5-7 business days and overnight delivery is available for an additional fee.

Sometimes account histories for other individuals are mistakenly included in your report, especially if you have a common last name. If you are a "Jr" and your father has the same name, sometimes you can mistakenly inherit his credit history. Mistaken identity can work for you or against you, depending on the individual whose credit you mistakenly inherit, so dispute any derogatory information that is not yours. If there is derogatory information on your credit report that belongs to your spouse or you are divorced, you can request to have a credit report that is in your name only. This will only work if you were not listed as a co-applicant on the account. Otherwise, derogatory information may carry-over to your individual credit report.

Bring your accounts current

If you are delinquent on your accounts, you should bring them up to date as soon as possible. Delinquency weighs heavily against your credit score because creditors believe that past history is reflective of future expectancy. Contact your creditors and make arrangements to make up the arrears on your obligations. Some creditors have "in house" programs through which they will bring you current after making a specified amount of consistent payments, regardless of whether you make up the arrears (this is known as reaging).

Voluntarily close your accounts

When you voluntarily close an account, the creditor is responsible for reporting it to the credit bureau and it should be documented on your credit report as "closed by consumer." The fact that you took the initiative in closing the account is an indication that you understand how to maintain reasonable use of credit and you are in control of your spending. After notifying a creditor that you want to close your account, you should always ask a creditor to provide a letter confirming that the account was reported to the credit bureau as "closed by consumer." By doing so, you can easily have it corrected if you later find that it is reported incorrectly on your credit report.

To optimize their credit score, consumers must maintain open accounts, but the number of accounts should be limited. Credit scoring models rate against "Too many bank revolving accounts" and "Too few bank revolving accounts." Establishing a consistent timely payment history on one or two major credit cards and limited merchant cards (department store cards and gas cards) will help to build a sufficient credit history. It is wise to close as many merchant cards as possible, especially on accounts that you opened solely for the purpose of making large "one time" purchases. For example, if you opened a credit line with an electronics store to purchase a computer, you should voluntarily close the account when the balance on the computer has been paid off, especially if you have no need for any other merchandise from that store. Otherwise, the account would remain open, which indicates that there is a potential that you will charge more debt. Generally speaking, large amounts of available credit can weigh against your credit score. The higher the cumulative total of available credit, the riskier it is to lend to the consumer. If a consumer has easy access to large amounts of available credit, one spending spree can cause them to go from financial stability to financial trouble.

Another reason why you should consider closing unnecessary charge accounts is because revolving debt (credit card debt) weighs heavier against your credit score than installment loan debt. Installment loan debt is debt that credit grantors underwrite (review for approval) each time a consumer requests an extension of credit. It is considered to be more regulated and consumers are less likely to get into a difficult financial situation because if they are risky to lend to, the loan will be denied. However, revolving debt is relatively easy to acquire by the consumer and if a consumer has high available balances on revolving debt, regulating use of their credit is at their own discretion, not the lenders. High credit limits on revolving debt may indicate a consumer's inability to control their spending behaviors. Successfully managing revolving debt is necessary to build credit but too much revolving debt may negatively affect your credit worthiness.

Pay down loan and credit card balances

If your balances are high relative to the loaned amount or credit limit, it may weigh against your credit score. High balances in comparison to your credit limit may be considered a sign that you are overextending yourself and dependent on credit to maintain, or artificially enhance, your style of living. It can be regarded as an indication that you are not in control of your spending habits because you consume up to the maximum that your credit will allow. If you pay your credit cards off on a monthly basis or carry reasonable balances and establish a consistent payment history on credit cards, it may assist you in building credit. However, carrying high balances and exhausting available credit limits may be considered unreasonable use of credit and may weigh against your credit score. Having too many accounts with balances on them may also weigh against your score.

Limit the number of new accounts and inquiries.

An excessive number of new accounts (accounts opened within the last year) or inquiries may indicate that a consumer is desperate for credit, which may be reflective of a credit problem. Too many new accounts can weigh against your credit score. Numerous inquiries may be considered a threat to a lender because they may indicate that a consumer is attempting to acquire multiple lines of credit at the same time, which could lead to the consumer being overextended and at risk of defaulting on their obligations. In accordance with the Fair Credit Reporting Act, inquiries can remain on a consumer's credit for a maximum of two years . Numerous inquiries may be reflective of a consumer who is subject to excessive impulse buying desires or a consumer that is dependent on additional credit to get out of a financial crisis.

Credit scoring is based, partially, on the maturity of the credit lines that are on a consumer's report. Accounts that have been established for years with a good payment history and reasonable use of available credit can stabilize and improve a credit score. However, accounts that are less than a year old, do not have a mature history and may weigh against the score because the consumer's ability to maintain long term stability with their increased spending power has not been established. Derogatory information that is reported on a consumer that has a mature history may not weigh against the credit score as much as derogatory information that is reported on a consumer who's credit history is not mature.

Pay off accounts that are public records, "charge-offs" and collection accounts.

Make arrangements to pay on accounts that have been charged off or placed in collections. Negotiating a settlement (see "Settling Debts," page 62) on collection accounts may be a very effective way of paying balances off at reduced amounts. If you have collection accounts, judgments, or tax liens, you should pay them off as soon as you can, depending on how close you are to having the accounts drop off of your credit report. Balances on tax liens and judgements are recorded as public record and have been deemed by the courts as legally owed by the debtor. Unsatisfied public records are considered good indicators that a debtor is not financially responsible and will weigh heavily against their credit score. Be sure that no information exceeds the reporting time-frame limitations as set forth by the Fair Credit Reporting Act.

ESTABLISHING BETTER CREDIT

Adopt the "friends and family" approach.

The concept of the "friends and family" approach is that you "assume" the good credit rating that a trusting friend or family member has already established. One way of doing this is to have a friend or family member call their credit card company and allow you to be listed on their credit card as a joint applicant. The credit card issuer will send you a card in the mail. A credit card company will submit a report to the credit reporting agencies and your report will be updated with the positive payment record that your friend has accumulated over the years. As your friend continues to charge on his card and pay faithfully, he will continue to build credit for you. You may want to consider taking the same approach with other cards or with other friends. Arrange in advance to "cut the credit card up" or return it to your friend or family member when you receive it in the mail.

If your credit is not sufficient enough to be approved for a loan with good terms, you can build credit by having a friend or family member cosign on a loan for you. When you are approved, you can arrange for the friend or family member to control the loaned amount so as to avoid any repayment complications. Your friend or family member can take the loaned amount and put it in a savings or money market account, or invest it as they see fit so the account will earn interest. They can repay the loan out of that account to ensure that you do not cause financial hardship or credit damage to them. You may have to make an arrangement with the cosigner to pay for the additional interest that you are charged on the loan if the return on their investment does not overcome the interest that is charged. If you have a trusting friend or family member and you are confident that you will be able to repay the loan, you can use the funds to refinance higher interest rate debt.

> *WHEN ADOPTING THE "FRIENDS AND FAMILY" APPROACH, IT IS BEST TO BE HONEST AND UP-FRONT WITH THE PERSON FROM WHOM YOU ARE ASSUMING THE GOOD CREDIT. IF YOU VIOLATE A FRIEND OR FAMILY MEMBER'S TRUST, NOT ONLY WILL YOU LOSE A CHANCE TO HELP REPAIR YOUR CREDIT, YOU MAY EVEN LOSE A TRUSTING FRIEND.*

Obtain a secured credit card.

If your credit has been damaged and you have been turned down for a conventional credit card, you will probably be able to obtain a secured card. Secured credit cards are usually available to debtors with even the worst credit. The idea behind a secured card is very similar to that of a secured loan, but it does not involve personal property. Instead of offering personal property as collateral, you will be required to forward money to the secured card issuer, who will place the money in a "deposit account" which earns interest. In return, they will give you a credit line that equals, or is a percentage of, the amount that you deposited (some creditors will issue a credit line larger than the deposit.) The creditor retains a security interest in the funds that you deposited and on the interest that the deposit earns and you will have to give up all control of the funds that you initially deposit. In most cases, a return of your deposit will only occur when your account has been paid in full and your, inactive, card has been returned to the issuer.

Before acquiring a secured card, you should make sure that the issuer will report your payment history to the credit bureau, just like any other credit card would. You should also make sure that the card is not reported to the credit bureau as "secured" by the credit issuer. Secured credit cards offer relatively low credit lines (usually from $200 to $500.) They should be used for the purpose of rebuilding credit and there should be no need for high credit limits that allow discretionary spending to grow out of control. Typically there is an annual membership fee and the interest rates are high (18-20%). Secured cards offer creditors and debtors a win-win situation if the debtor uses them correctly. There is minimal risk to the lender because if you default on your obligation to repay the money that they loaned to you, they can take your security deposit, guaranteeing them a return on the principal amount that they loaned you. Additionally, they will have made money on any interest and fees that you paid prior to defaulting on your obligation. You get to have the convenience of a credit card while you are rebuilding your credit and learning new budgeting skills.

Obtain a merchant card.

Apply for cards from retail stores or gasoline companies. Department store and gas cards are usually easier to qualify for. They are usually more liberal concerning approval on lines of credit. Tire stores, jewelry stores, furniture stores, and appliance stores are other good sources for "easier" credit. The credit limit that they approve is normally lower than a major credit card would offer, but making reasonable monthly charges and paying consistent monthly payments on them will enable you to reestablish credit. Establishing credit will help you to qualify for major credit cards with higher credit limits that will build even more credit for you.

CHAPTER 8

LOANS: UNSECURED PERSONAL AND HOME EQUITY LOANS

CHAPTER 8

LOANS: UNSECURED PERSONAL
AND HOME EQUITY LOANS

Unsecured Signature Loans

Consumers who are experiencing difficulty with their finances sometimes turn to signature loans for help. Signature loans can be an effective answer to debt problems, but they are not always the most economical solution. Unsecured signature loans are loans that are not backed by collateral such as a car, home or other personal property. They are referred to as "signature" loans because a consumer's signature is all that is required to back them. Unsecured loans are considered higher risk loans because there is nothing of value placed against the loan to offset the possibility that the consumer may default on repayment. The interest rates are considerably higher due to the increased risk and due to the fact that collecting on the money in the event of default is difficult and timely, if not impossible.

In most cases, acquiring an unsecured loan to consolidate debt is only economical for consumers who have very good credit that will enable them to qualify for a reasonable interest rate. Most likely, consumers who have a lot of debt or who have questionable credit will not be approved for unsecured loans at terms that benefit them. If they are approved, they will be offered the loan at a relatively high interest rate that does not offer reasonable savings in comparison to the interest rate on the bills that they are trying to consolidate. Due to the fact that the terms of repayment of unsecured loans are usually relatively short (usually 3-5 years) and interest rates are relatively high; payments on unsecured loans can be large and burdensome. When shopping for signature loans, consumers should compare interest rates and be sure that their monthly payment will comfortably fit into their budget.

Where to go for unsecured signature loans

If you are interested in obtaining a signature loan to consolidate existing debt, you can go to a local bank, your credit union, or a finance company. If you belong to a credit union, you may be able to qualify for a lower rate loan with good terms because of your membership. Credit unions may be more lenient when evaluating a consumer's credit because there is a better member-banker relation. Another good source for signature loans are local banks. Your success in obtaining a loan with good rates may be dependent, in part, on your relationship with the bank but banks usually offer relatively low interest rates on signature loans. Typically, banks and credit unions offer interest rates that vary from 10% to 15% (depending on the rate at which they can borrow money to lend to consumers).

If you have not had success in obtaining a loan from a traditional bank or credit union, you may be able to qualify for a loan through a finance company. Be very careful when considering a loan from a finance company. Individuals who have excessive debt or questionable credit find more success in acquiring signature loans through finance companies, but the loans often come with a big price tag. Signature loans are risky because they are unsecured and when combined with questionable credit worthiness, they become even more risky to lenders. Due to the increased risk, finance company interest rates can be very high (sometimes more than 25%). Higher interest means higher payments that may contribute to mismanagement of finances and overextension of consumer credit. Finance company loans may be regarded as indicators that the consumer has exhausted conventional options and is desperate for credit. Finance company debt weighs against credit scoring models because, it may be reflective of a consumer who is dependent on high interest credit to continue adverse spending behavior.

96

Equity Loans

Equity loans are loans that consumers take out against the value of their home. For consumers to benefit from equity loans, they must realize that they are not a "quick fix" but can be very effective in assisting to reduce debt when combined with sound planning, repayment strategy, and budgeting. The fact that equity loans are backed by the value of a consumer's home makes them less risky to the lender because they can recoup most of their assets in the event of foreclosure. The relatively low risk of lending enables banks to offer more favorable interest rates. Home equity lenders have guidelines that dictate the interest rates that they offer. One major determining factor is the amount of the loan in comparison to the value of the home. Generally speaking, the higher the "loan to value" percentage, the higher the interest rate will be on the loan. Another very important factor is the consumer's credit score. The better the credit score, the more options the consumer will be able to be approved for. A consumer who has a good credit score will have an easier time being qualified and will be able to qualify for riskier loans. Most likely, they will be able to obtain better interest rates on their loan.

Equity loans are becoming increasingly popular in today's credit society because, not only do they allow consumers to borrow at relatively low interest rates, they are installment loans that can be repaid over a relatively long period of time. Lower interest rates and the longer pay back periods enable consumers to have lower, more manageable payments that reduce the stress on the consumer's budget. Equity loans allow the consumer to pay off high interest, revolving credit accounts on which interest is charged on interest that has already accrued. The interest that a consumer pays on the money that they borrow against the value of their home can be deducted from their income tax. Despite all of the positive aspects, the world of equity lending is a very dangerous and confusing world for debtors who find themselves amidst financial trouble. The debtor must understand that equity loans do not simply eliminate debt or make it disappear, they simply "reshuffle" the payoff time frame and the interest in a manner that makes payments easier to afford. When considering a home equity loan, you must use caution and change your spending behavior accordingly.

Equity Loans: Jekyll or Hyde

If you watch television, you cannot help but notice that equity loan commercials are everywhere. As a way of establishing consumer trust, the banks hire public figures such as your favorite sports stars to promote the benefits of acquiring a home equity loan to get out of debt. They also emphasize the benefit of being able to write the interest off. However, they forget to tell troubled consumers that equity loans are a good solution to their problems, only if they have adjusted their view of credit and their spending behavior. Much like determining whether credit is "good" or "evil," determining whether equity loans are "Jekyll" or "Hyde" is dependent on the behavior that consumers exhibit after acquiring them.

As a solution to troubled finances, consumers should approach equity loans with cautious enthusiasm. The truth is, equity loans can be a debtor's saving grace, but they can also be their worst nightmare. When combined with household budgeting and a repayment plan, acquiring a home equity loan can be an extremely effective tool that offers instant payment relief and eliminates debt relatively quickly. When combined with poor budgeting and continued irresponsible spending habits, acquiring a home equity loan will simply be a short-term, quick fix that creates a false sense of security for the consumer and leads to more irrational spending. Troubled debtors who are forced to turn to equity loans, and do not adjust the habits that caused them to have to depend on the loans, often overextend themselves and allow their finances to live on borrowed time.

Understanding How Equity Loans Work

The equity that you have in your home is calculated by subtracting the amount that you still owe on your mortgage(s) from the value of your home. For purposes of illustration, let's assume that the John Doe owns a home that is worth $100,000 and he still owes $55,000 on his mortgage. John's mortgage payment is $730 and he has a 9% interest rate on his mortgage loan. He has $15,000 worth of credit card debt with 19% interest and his minimum payments are $325 per month. He has a car loan with a balance of $10,000 at 10% interest on which the payments are $300.00 per month. John worked out his budget and feels that he cannot successfully manage his finances any longer if he does not reduce his expenditures.

John would have $45,000 worth of equity in his home. (Value ($100,000) minus amount owed ($55,000)).

Mortgage Refinance

Most home mortgage refinances allow consumers to borrow up to 80% of the value of their home. Using the example above, John would be able to borrow up to $80,000 (80% of $100,000). If he refinanced his mortgage, John could pay the balance that he owed on his old mortgage ($55,000) and use the remaining available equity ($25,000), to pay off his credit cards ($15,000) and car ($10,000).

Using the example above, let's say John could refinance at 7.5% as opposed to the 9% that he is currently paying. Not only would John be able to save 1.5% (9%-7.5%) on the balance that he rewrote on his mortgage, he would be able to save 11.5% interest (19%-7.5%) by paying off his credit cards. Additionally, he would save 2.5% interest (10%-7.5%) on his car.

John's total monthly expenditures before the rewrite are as follows:

$730 first mortgage
$300 car payment
$325 credit card payments
$1,355 total

Assuming John did a 30-year mortgage refinance, after paying off his bills by rewriting his mortgage at 7.5%, his total monthly expenditures would be $559.37 (paid off $55,000 existing mortgage, $10,000 car, and $15,000 credit cards).

John will save $795.63 in monthly expenditures

Second Mortgage

As opposed to doing a complete rewrite of his mortgage, John would have the option of taking a second mortgage. A second mortgage would allow John to take a second loan against the value of his home that remains after accounting for the balance owed on the first mortgage. Second mortgages allow consumers to borrow up to 100% of the value of the home and sometimes more (see over-equity loans below). Using the example above, if John had more credit card debt (let's say $35,000 worth with a monthly payment of $775) the value of his home would not be enough to cover his bills at 80% loan to value on a first mortgage refinance. However, on a second mortgage, John could borrow up to 100% loan to value and he could take a second loan out for the available equity ($45,000) to pay off his credit cards and car. Assuming, John got a 30 year second mortgage at 11% and, with it, he paid off his credit cards ($35,000) and his car loan ($10,000):

John would reduce the interest that he was paying on his credit cards by 8%(19%-11%). He would have 1% higher interest on his car but it would ease the payment burden, which will allow John to stay in control of his finances.

Before the second mortgage, John's monthly expenditures would be as follows:

$730 first mortgage
$300 car loan
$775 credit cards

$1,805 total

After acquiring his second mortgage, John's monthly expenditures would be as follows:

$730   first mortgage
$428.55 second mortgage (paid off $10,000 car and $35,000
                                              credit cards)

$1,158.55 total

John saves $646.45 in monthly expenditures.

Over-equity loans.

Today's world of home equity loans is a much more liberal one in which lenders allow consumers to have more borrowing power. As opposed to conventional second mortgage lending, through which a consumer can borrow 80-100% against the value of their home, today's lenders allow debtors to borrow up to 125% of the value of their home. Generally speaking, the higher the percentage value of the home that is being loaned, the higher the interest rate that is charged on the balance. These higher-risk loans are often called Over-equity Loans or "125's" and the interest rate on them is considerably higher. Using the example above, if John Doe was able to qualify for an over-equity loan, he may be able to borrow up to a total of $125,000 ($25,000 more than the value of his home). Over-equity loans can be helpful to consumers who need to reduce the burden of high monthly payment expenditures and desire to refinance debt amounts that exceed the value of their home.

For purposes of illustrating the benefits of over-equity loans, let's suppose John had $55,000 worth of credit card debt and he had to pay $1200 per month in minimum payments. A conventional mortgage refinance or second mortgage would not allow John to pay off all of his credit cards. The difference between the value of his home ($100,000) and the balance that he owed on his mortgage $55,000 would only leave him a maximum $45,000 of home value to borrow against. If John could not pay off his credit cards, he feels he will have to file bankruptcy because he cannot afford to pay his minimum payments on his credit cards and pay his other expenses. John really does not want to file bankruptcy. If he was approved for an over-equity loan, he could have up to $70,000 ($125,000 (125% value of his home)- $55,000 first mortgage) worth of borrowing power to pay off his credit cards. If the interest rate on John's over-equity loan is 14%, and John paid off his credit cards ($55,000) and car ($10,000), the effect of the loan on John's monthly expenditures would be as follows:

Before the over-equity loan, John's expenditures would be as follows:

$730 First mortgage
$1200 Credit cards
$300 Car
_____
$2230 total

If he took a 20-year over-equity loan at 14%, John's expenditures would be as follows:

$730   First mortgage
$808.29 Payment on over-equity loan (paid off $10,000 car and
$55,000 credit cards)
_____
$1538.29 total

John will save $691.71 in monthly expenditures.

101

Important factors to account for when considering a home equity loan.

1) The higher the amount of the loan in comparison to the value of the home, the higher the interest rate you will be charged.
2) The interest that you pay on the amount of money that you borrowed up to the value of your home is tax deductible. However, the amount of money that you borrow above and beyond the value of your home is usually not tax deductible (consult your tax accountant for advice).
3) Refinancing your home allows you to take debts on which you cannot deduct the interest on your taxes (credit cards, cars, personal loans), and convert it into debt on which you can deduct the interest on your taxes. However, refinancing may turn unsecured debt into debt that is secured by your home. If you fall behind on unsecured debt there is no risk of your property being taken from you. However, your home is likely to be foreclosed upon in the event of default on mortgage loan payments.
4) The closing costs that you pay on your loan can offset the interest that you save. Closing costs may include attorney, appraisal, recording, title, mortgage insurance, credit report, and origination fees. As a rule of thumb, the higher the loan amount to the value of the home, the higher the loan costs. Lenders are required to provide you with a Truth in Lending Statement that demonstrates the effective APR (annual percentage rate). The APR will account for closing costs that you pay on the loan. Always read the Truth in Lending Statement.
5) Repayment options on home equity loans range from 15-30 years. The longer the term on the loan, the lower the payment but the more interest the debtor will pay over time. The terms of repayment on a home equity loan should be as short as the debtor can possibly afford without risking a payment that is too high and does not allow for the debtor to pay other expenses.
6) Beware of loans with prepayment penalties. Some loans carry penalties that are as much as six months worth of interest if the loan is paid off ahead of schedule. If possible, avoid loans with prepayment penalties.

7) When refinancing your mortgage, you may have the option of an Adjustable Rate Mortgage (ARM) or a Fixed Rate Mortgage. Generally speaking, the starting interest rate on an adjustable rate mortgage is lower than a Fixed Rate Mortgage. ARM interest rate adjustments fluctuate based on the prime rate (The interest rate at which lenders can borrow from the federal government.) After periodic adjustments (usually yearly) the interest rate on an ARM can exceed the fixed interest rate that you would have obtained. If you choose an ARM and your timing is right, your interest rate may never exceed the interest that you would have gotten on a fixed rate mortgage.

John Doe— Financial Wizard or Financial Fool?

In all of the John Doe examples above, it appears that John can do no wrong. He paid his high interest credit card debt off at a lower interest rate by using the value of his home. He also reduced his payments and no longer has to feel stressed out about falling behind. Additionally, John can now write off the interest that he pays on the amount that he has financed up to the value of his home and he has alleviated the total amount of debt payment that he pays each month. Not to mention the fact that he now has an installment loan that paid off his revolving credit card accounts that were driving up the effective rate of his interest.

John is a financial guru, right?—Maybe!

John's decision to refinance his credit card debt is only as good as his ability to curb his spending habits. John now has extra money each month and things are not as stressful on him. However, if he uses the money the wrong way, he may be adding to the snowball effect that started when he first began to acquire too much credit by making only the minimum monthly payments. Suppose a sudden life-changing event occurred that required financial reserves to get him through. If John or his spouse lost their job, would he be able to maintain his mortgage payment(s)?

John should immediately tear his credit cards up to ensure that he is not making his situation worse by charging up more debt. If he assumes more debt, he will have to pay more in monthly payments to service the debt and he will find himself "living on the edge" again. This time, there will be no equity or value in his home to use. To add to the dilemma, all of John's debt will now be secured by the value of his home and if he cannot afford the payment on his mortgage(s) he may risk being foreclosed upon. If John continues to use the disposable income that the home loan made available for discretionary spending, he will be borrowing against time and eventually, he will probably have to "pay the piper."

If John were to gain from his home loan he would have to use his disposable income constructively. On a monthly basis, he would take a small portion and put it into savings to prepare for "a rainy day." He would take another larger portion of the disposable income and repay it into his mortgage(s) to shorten the term of the home loan(s) and save himself interest. John might even invest a portion of his monthly savings for retirement. As opposed to viewing his disposable income as a vehicle that will allow him to spend more, he should use it as a resource to get him further out of debt. John should realize that his situation is not going to take care of itself and that he needs to take proactive steps to get out of debt. He should understand that 25-30 years is a long time during which to pay back a loan and the longer he takes to pay it off, the more interest he pays to the bank. If John combines budgeting and strategic financial planning with the other benefits that the home loan brings to the table for him, he will probably be on the road to recovery. Just like any other form of debt reduction, John's efforts are going to require organization, commitment, sacrifice, and patience.

If you are current on your bills, own a home and are interested in a home equity loan to consolidate your bills, contact:

F&M Mortgage Services, Inc.
A subsidiary of F&M Bank-Winchester

(800) 955-0031

They offer many different equity loan options.

CHAPTER 9

CREDIT COUNSELING

CHAPTER 9

CREDIT COUNSELING

UNDERSTANDING CREDIT COUNSELING PROGRAMS

If you have not been able to create a workable budget and stick to it, cannot work out a payment plan on your own with your creditors, or cannot keep track of bills that continuously stack up, credit counseling may help. Counseling may also help if you are opposed to the idea of taking another loan or line of credit to get out of debt, or if your credit is prohibiting you from getting a loan. Counseling agencies do not place loans for consumers. Instead, they offer programs through which they will work with you to establish a repayment plan that is agreeable to both you and your creditors. In most cases, credit counseling agencies can only obtain more favorable repayment terms on unsecured debts such as credit cards, collection debts, medical bills and unsecured loans. They are most successful at helping you with credit card debt and they require that you stop using your line(s) of credit.

Most credit counseling agencies offer budgeting assistance and budgeting tips that often prove very useful for troubled debtors. They often act as the helpful partner that a consumer needs to help them stay on the road to becoming debt free. A counseling agency will negotiate with your creditors in an attempt to get them to reduce your interest rates and reduce monthly expenditures. They often request voluntary contributions to help offset the costs of providing the repayment service for debtors. Counseling agencies are often successful in getting credit card and loan companies to stop charging costly penalty fees such as late and over-limit fees. For debtors who are behind on their obligations, they can often arrange with some creditors to have their accounts re-aged or brought back to a current status as they are reported on a credit report. However, this does not mean that the agency will "erase" marks that are preexisting on a debtor's credit report. The criteria for bringing the accounts current, differs from creditor to creditor. Counseling plans can be very effective in eliminating the stress that is caused by creditors and assist in establishing a consistent payment pattern which may help a consumer who is at risk of being sued by his creditors. Credit Counselors are often trained to advise debtors of their rights under the Fair Debt Collection Practices Act and the Fair Credit Reporting Act. After assisting you with your budget, they will send proposals to your creditors as a means of getting your creditors to accept the new, more favorable, repayment terms.

Generally speaking, the credit counseling agency calculates your payment based on predetermined criteria that the creditors require. The creditors will only accept the proposals and give better repayment benefits if the proposed payment meets their criteria. When enrolled in a counseling plan, you send payments to the counseling agency, who then distributes the payments to the creditors to have them applied at the more favorable rates. It is your responsibility to get payments to the counseling agency on time. If you are late with payments to the agency, your payments will usually still be applied at the lower interest rates but penalty fees may still be applied and your account may not be brought back to a current status. Typically, repayment plans will enable consumers to get out of debt in 3-6 years. Credit counseling has proven to be an effective way of reestablishing credit and saving debtors a lot of money in interest and penalties.

A debtor's responsibility when on a counseling program

- Provide creditor information to the agency, including the name of the creditor, the address, the account number, the balance, and the type of debt.
- Provide information about their household budget.
- Make payments on time and in full each month.
- Monitor their monthly statements to verify that payments are being applied on time.
- Where applicable, the debtor is responsible for monitoring their monthly statements to ensure that their interest rates have been

reduced, penalty fees are not being applied, and the accounts have been brought to a current status.
- Advise the agency when an account has been paid off.
- Remove credit insurance on credit card accounts.

FREQUENTLY ASKED QUESTIONS

Is credit counseling considered to be bankruptcy?

Credit counseling is not bankruptcy. It is considered an effective alternative to bankruptcy. Credit counseling programs are similar to Chapter 13 bankruptcy only by the fact that they are a repayment plan. When a consumer files bankruptcy, creditors are often forced to discharge debt and the consumer is no longer held legally liable for the debt. If a client files chapter 13, the creditors are forced to accept the repayment terms that are established. They are also forced to accept the fact that the debtor can repay unsecured debt at a fraction of the dollar amount owed. Credit counseling is a repayment plan that is mutually agreed upon by the creditors and the consumer. As opposed to reducing the amount of debt that is owed by the consumer, the creditors make adjustments in interest rates and penalty fees that enable the consumer to repay the debt at an accelerated pace. The program will enable the creditor to recoup all of the funds that were loaned to the debtor. Counseling programs are not forced upon the creditor like bankruptcy and the client still maintains legal liability for repayment of the debt, which limits the effect that it will have on the consumer's credit.

How will being on a credit counseling program effect my credit?

Credit counseling exists to assist creditors in collecting debts and assisting debtors in preserving credit. It is a plan that can only work if the creditors cooperate, which most of them do. However, the creditors reserve the right to report to the credit bureau that the debtor's account with them is enrolled on a credit counseling program. In rare cases, creditors may report that you are late on payment obligations. However, most creditors view credit counseling as an acceptable alternative to reducing the burden of debt, or they would not agree to adjust the repayment terms. For debtors who are behind on their payment obligations, most creditors will arrange to bring them current after enrolling in a counseling program.

How much does it cost to enroll in a credit counseling program?

When searching for a credit counseling organization to assist you, you should look for a nonprofit organization. Most nonprofit counseling agencies do not charge fees. However, they do ask for voluntary contributions to offset their administrative costs and the costs that they incur when negotiating with creditors and establishing an account for a debtor. There are for-profit organizations that perform counseling services, but they usually charge large fees. Generally speaking, for-profit counseling agencies are unable to get the creditors to agree to repayment benefits that are as favorable as the benefits that nonprofit agencies are able to arrange.

Can I still use my credit cards when I am on a counseling program?

As part of the mutual agreement between the creditors and the client, the client is required to stop using the charge cards. Acquiring more debt while trying to get out of debt, defeats the purpose of the program. If the creditors are willing to give more favorable repayment benefits, they want to make sure that the client cannot charge more debt. The creditors close the accounts and sometimes request that the debtor cut the card up or send it back to them. Reinstatement of charging privileges is done at the creditor's discretion.

CHAPTER 10

BANKRUPTCY: THE LAST RESORT

CHAPTER 10

BANKRUPTCY: THE LAST RESORT

Bankruptcy can be a good solution for individuals who have tried other methods of debt resolution and have experienced no relief. Sometimes a debtor has tried budgeting, refinancing is not an option, and credit counseling has even proven ineffective because the consumer cannot afford to pay the bills through the counseling company and still meet other obligations. After being forced into a "rob Peter to pay Paul" last ditch effort, the debtor realizes that they need salvation. Often, debtor's finances are stacked against them. Limited financial resources cause a situation in which attempts to handle the debt is just prolonging the agony and making it nearly impossible to effectively satisfy all of their obligations. Bankruptcy may be the only effective alternative to dealing with the tension and emotional distress that are created by the financial hopelessness. When a consumer files bankruptcy, they are protected from the emotional distress of collection attempts because the creditors must obey an automatic stay that requires them to cease any collection activity, including telephone calls, bills, and even law suits that are pending against them. Each bankruptcy case is assigned a court appointed trustee who acts as an intermediary and is responsible for seeing that the creditors re-cooperate as much as possible within the legal limits of the bankruptcy court.

The decision to file bankruptcy is one that should be thought out thoroughly. Many consumers learn, only after filing, that it has lasting negative effects that limit financial options and ability to obtain credit.

Many bankruptcy attorneys are overzealous in their approach to soliciting the benefits of bankruptcy because they earn money by helping consumers file. Likewise, in their pursuit of money, aggressive collectors scare consumers, who are unaware of their legal rights, into unnecessarily filing bankruptcy. Often, consumers realize that the long-term sacrifices created by the lasting effects of filing bankruptcy outweigh the pain that the collectors were causing. In many cases, if the debtor had "called the collector's bluff" and simply ignored the threats, they would have realized that they were unfounded.

Instead of viewing it as a last resort, many consumers view bankruptcy as a "get out of debtor's prison free card" that can be redeemed when debt repayment gets too difficult. Bankruptcy can help consumers get out of debtor's prison but it certainly comes with a price. Viewing bankruptcy as an easy way out can cause extremely poor spending habits by consumers who fail to face the reality of their financial mismanagement and fall right back into the same situation. Bankruptcy often carries long term derogatory effects on credit and successful future financial management and understanding. Individuals who view bankruptcy as an easy way out, often fail to learn from their mistakes and continue to exhibit the adverse spending behaviors that created their problem in the first place. Bankruptcy should be viewed as a right and not a privilege. Many consumers who want to file, learn after assuming massive amounts of debt, that it will not all be dismissed. There are different types of bankruptcy, each having its own guidelines and limitations. Financial circumstances often prohibit consumers from instantaneously eliminating all of their debt through bankruptcy.

THE LINGERING EFFECTS OF BANKRUPTCY

Though bankruptcy may be a very good solution to a severe financial problem, filing carries negative effects that follow a debtor for a relatively long time. The debtor may lose property that is nonexempt (unprotected) and have to start over again in fulfilling life long goals. Bankruptcy will appear on a consumer's credit report for seven to ten years depending on which type of bankruptcy is filed. Chapter 7 will normally be reported for ten years because it does not involve any form of repayment plan to creditors and debts are completely discharged. Chapter 13 may carry less of a stigma and often appears for only seven years on a debtor's credit file because the debtor arranges to repay a portion of their debt. Filing bankruptcy carries a negative stigma because it is viewed, by some, as an indication that an individual does not know how to live up to their financial obligations. However, bankruptcy gives consumers the ability to "wipe the slate clean" and start over again. The aftereffects of bankruptcy are severe and require reestablishment of "creditor confidence," which often takes a long time. Bankruptcy may be a relatively quick and easy solution to financial woes, but it is also a quick way to severely damage credit worthiness. Repairing credit often requires a considerable amount of time and there is no simple solution to damaged credit.

Often, consumers who are in the process of rebounding from filing bankruptcy and reestablishing credit, suffer financial penalties as a result. Acquiring additional credit is very difficult and if the consumer is granted credit, they may be penalized by the interest rate that they have to pay on the money that is loaned to them. Obtaining unsecured lines of credit, such as conventional credit cards, is extremely difficult, if not impossible, immediately after filing bankruptcy because there is no collateral to offset the risk of loaning money. Since filing bankruptcy is the most drastic measure that can be taken as a solution to debt problems, most creditors consider lending to consumers who filed bankruptcy, a very risky proposition. Due to the increased risk in lending to individuals who have filed bankruptcy, the interest rate that the creditor will grant to bankruptcy filers can be significantly higher (sometimes double). Over time, the high interest rates will cost the consumer a lot of money and will drive the consumer's monthly payment obligations up considerably. Creditors are less reluctant to lend to consumers on secured lines of credit because the collateral helps offset the risk of lending to an individual who has filed bankruptcy. If the consumer defaults on the loan, the creditor can foreclose upon or repossess the collateral.

THE PROCESS OF FILING BANKRUPTCY

Title 11 of the United States Bankruptcy Code governs bankruptcy proceedings and bankruptcy is a matter of public record. To file bankruptcy, you must first file a bankruptcy petition. You must also complete schedules of assets and liabilities, and prepare a statement of financial affairs. These forms will require you to list your property and account for recent sales of personal property. They also require you to list your income, the debts that you owe, and account for any money that you spent during the two-year period prior to filing. You must list all of your debts on the bankruptcy petition. The bankruptcy court will require that you pay a filing fee, which is approximately $175. The filing fee is separate from the fees that a consumer pays to their personal bankruptcy attorney for representation and guidance in filing.

In Chapter 7 cases, the debtor is required to attend at least one meeting of creditors, during which, they may be questioned, under oath, by a court appointed bankruptcy trustee and the creditors about their finances. In Chapter 13 cases, the debtor may be required to attend multiple meetings with the creditors to work out a repayment plan in detail. A valuation hearing may be needed if the creditors are in disagreement with the value of the assets that the debtor listed on their schedules. During a bankruptcy proceeding, if a creditor suspects that a consumer is withholding information or has hidden or transferred assets to other individuals, they are entitled to question the debtor at the meeting(s) of creditors. The creditor reserves the right to file an adversary proceeding if they feel that a claim is non-dischargeable. Typically, a creditor will file an adversary proceeding against claims involving criminal misconduct such as debts incurred on the basis of fraud or larceny, breach of trust or embezzlement, or debts from willful or malicious injury to another person or their property. The creditor may also file an adversary proceeding against damages arising from drunk driving obligations. The trustee will be particularly interested in determining if the filer is attempting to abuse the bankruptcy system.

The trustee will be particularly interested in determining the following:

- If there are any assets that are nonexempt
- If the debtor has concealed or transferred assets
- If the debtor ran up debts prior to filing
- If the debtor used false information on credit applications to obtain credit

116

IF A DEBTOR IS FOUND GUILTY OF MISCONDUCT, THEIR DEBTS WILL NOT BE DISCHARGED FOR THAT FILING OR FOR ANY FUTURE BANKRUPTCY PROCEEDINGS. ADDITIONALLY, THE TRUSTEE MAY ATTEMPT TO RECOVER ANY ASSETS THAT WERE TRANSFERRED OUT OF THEIR NAME AND LIQUIDATION OF THEIR ASSETS MAY CONTINUE FOR THE BENEFIT OF THE CREDITORS TO WHOM THE DEBTOR MUST REPAY THE DEBT.

THE MOST COMMON FORMS OF BANKRUPTCY

Chapter 7 Bankruptcy

Chapter 7 is otherwise known as "straight bankruptcy" and is considered to be the "quick fix" solution to eliminating debt. The debtor is allowed to retain all assets that are considered exempt assets. Filing Chapter 7 may require that the courts liquidate the value of nonexempt personal property. This means that the trustee may sell unprotected personal property to repay the creditors who loaned money to the debtor. Nonexempt assets may include collateral such as a house, car, or land that the debtor used to secure a loan. There are limitations from state to state that determine what personal property may be exempted but Chapter 7 provides adequate protection for most assets.

Chapter 7 is best for debtors who have excessive unsecured debt because it completely eliminates the debtor's legal liability and responsibility for repaying unsecured debt. However, if the debtor is behind on secured debt (debt involving collateral), such as a home or car, it will not eliminate their obligation to repay the debt nor the amount that they fell behind. For Chapter 7 bankruptcies, the time frame from filing to receipt of discharge can usually take anywhere from three to five months. Discharge is when the bankruptcy court officially ends your case and dismisses you from the legal liability to repay the debts. Only debts that are listed on the bankruptcy petition forms and existed on the date that the bankruptcy was filed may be discharged. If a debtor desires to retain property that is secured by collateral, they will have to make acceptable arrangements to pay for it during or after the bankruptcy because the discharge does not eliminate the creditor's right to reclaim the property. It only prevents them from holding the debtor responsible for legal liability. In other words, if they take the property and sell it, and the proceeds do not cover the balance that is owed, they cannot hold the debtor responsible for the difference (their loss).

If a debtor files Chapter 7, the creditors may pursue any cosigner who agreed to accept legal liability for the debt. The creditors will probably require that the debtor signs a reaffirmation agreement if they desire to keep personal property that was used to secure a loan. Through the reaffirmation agreement, the creditors allow the debtor to keep the property, but the debtor agrees to remain legally liable for it. When a debtor reaffirms, they forfeit the automatic stay that protects them and the debtor and creditor then have the same rights and liabilities that they had before the bankruptcy was filed. After signing the reaffirmation agreement, if the debtor falls behind during or after the bankruptcy, the creditor can repossess the property and legally pursue the debtor for any losses that remain after selling the property.

Following are Debts that cannot be discharged through Chapter 7:

- *Credit card, personal loans, and installment purchases made within 40 days of filing*
- *Debts resulting from fraud*
- *Debts resulting from drinking and driving or reckless driving*
- *Fines from traffic tickets or debts that result from criminal negligence*
- *Debts from willful or malicious injury to another person or their property*
- *Alimony*
- *Child Support*
- *Student Loans*
  ➩*In 1998 the law changed with regard to discharge of student loans. Prior bankruptcy law allowed student loans to be discharged once they were seven years or older from the day they were first due. Currently, student loans cannot be discharged unless the debtor passes an undue hardship test. The debtor has to prove that a good faith effort was made to repay the loan and prove that a minimal standard of living cannot be maintained if forced to repay the loan(s). The guidelines of a "minimal standard of living" are very rigid and discharge of student loans under Chapter 7 is uncommon.*

• *Income Taxes*

⇨*Generally speaking, for taxes to be discharged, the following criteria must be met:*

1. *A tax return filed for the year in question was filed on time, or if not, then it was filed at least two years before the bankruptcy.*
2. *The tax is over three years old.*
3. *The tax was assessed more than eight months before the bankruptcy was filed.*
4. *The debtor did not willfully evade the tax.*

Chapter 13 Bankruptcy

Chapter 13 differs from Chapter 7 because it involves a repayment plan that is submitted to the trustee and the bankruptcy court for approval. The debtor is required to create a feasible monthly budget that will enable them to meet their basic needs and still be able to afford to make scheduled payments to the bankruptcy trustee. A formal plan is prepared and submitted with the bankruptcy petition to determine how much money will be repaid to the creditors through a deed trust payment each month. Chapter 13 permits a debtor to repay in monthly installments for three to five years and allows the debtor to keep all of their assets, even if their value exceeds the amount of the exemptions allowed by the state. Chapter 13 allows debtors to propose repayment of unsecured debts, such as credit cards, at a fraction of what was owed. You may maintain your secured assets because, over time, you will be repaying your creditors the amount that you had fallen delinquent. To qualify for Chapter 13, your unsecured debts must be less than $250,000 and your secured debts must total less than $750,000. In addition, you must have a stable and regular income.

If a debtor has considerable debts that may be liquidated and lost under Chapter 7, they may consider Chapter 13. Debts that would not be discharged under Chapter 7 can be included and retained under Chapter 13. For example, if a debtor's mortgage or auto payments are behind and they do not have the ability to bring them current, Chapter 13 may be the answer. It will allow the arrears to be paid back over a three to five year period and the creditors would not be permitted to repossess the vehicle, provided the debtor made the bankruptcy payments on time. Chapter 13 allows a debtor who was in arrears on federal income tax to establish a payment plan through which they can pay the IRS back over time. Under Chapter 13, the automatic stay will protect any cosigners on the consumer's debts. A Chapter 13 bankruptcy is not discharged until all deed trust payments have been made, which usually takes three to five years.

BANKRUPTCY COMPARISON CHART

The following charts (Figure 10.1) present a comparison summary of Chapter 7 and Chapter 13 Bankruptcy.

Figure 10.1 **Chapter 7**

Ideally suited for:	Chapter 7 is ideal for unsecured debt such as credit cards, medical bills, collection accounts and personal loans that are usually easily discharged. If you are at risk of losing personal property or have a lot of non-exempt assets that can be taken by the court, Chapter 13 may be a better option. If the bankruptcy court determines that you can repay your debt within a 3-5 year period, they can require that you file chapter 13.
Discharge of unsecured debt:	Unsecured debt is easily discharged and the debtor is no longer held legally liable for it.
Filing Requirements:	There are no guidelines with regard to amount of debt. If your debts were discharged through a Chapter 7 or Chapter 13 case that started within the last six years, you cannot file again.
Length of time from filing until discharge:	It usually takes approximately 3-6 months until the case is discharged.
Debtor's right to retain personal property:	Assets that are not exempt (personal property that you cannot legally keep) may be sold to repay the creditors. Exemption guidelines are determined by the state in which the bankruptcy is being filed but they usually allow for the client to retain most of their property. If the debtor is behind on secured loans, such as automobile or a mortgage payments and cannot catch up, they may lose their property. The debtor's legal liability will be discharged but the creditor still has the right to repossess any personal property. If the debtor wishes to retain personal property, he will probably be required to sign a reaffirmation agreement with the creditor. When a reaffirmation agreement is signed, the debtor may keep the property but must accept legal liability again. This gives the creditor the right to sue the client. Debtors who file chapter 7 should be sure that they bring their secured loans back to current and remain current on them or they may be repossessed.

Chapter 13

Chapter 13 is a repayment plan and it is ideal for debts that are not easily discharged under Chapter 7, such as taxes, alimony, or child support. Unlike Chapter 7, it can also include debts that were incurred by fraud, larceny, embezzlement, assault, battery, false imprisonment, or defamation. The repayment plan can include secured loans, such as a house or automobile, on which the debtor needs to make up delinquent payments or on which the debtor is at risk of losing personal property. Chapter 13 is ideal for avoiding law suits, judgements, attachment of personal property, and garnishments.

Most unsecured debt is discharged. Repayment of unsecured debt is usually done at a fraction the dollar amount owed. If a client has personal assets that exceed the amount of allowed exemptions, they may still keep their property. However, the dollar amount exceeding the amount of allowed exemptions must be re-paid through the payment plan.

The debtor must have a regular and disposable income. The maximum amount of unsecured debt that a debtor may have is $250,000. The maximum amount of secured debt that a debtor may have is $750,000.

It usually takes 3-5 years until the case is discharged. The case will not be discharged until all deed trust payments are made and the creditors have been re-paid.

The debtor will not lose personal property, regardless of whether their assets exceed exemptions, because they will be re-paid through the re-organizational payment plan. If the debtor is behind on payments to secured loans, the creditors cannot repossess personal property, even if they do not like the terms of repayment, because the debtor will be repaying the arrears over the course of the repayment plan.

Index

C